Artists
Dorothy Cameron
Ian Carr-Harris
Robin Collyer
Vera Frenkel
Myfanwy MacLeod
Sandra Meigs
Terry Pfliger

Telling Stories, Secret Lives

Jan Allen, Steven Matijcio

Writers
Jill Battson
Steven Heighton
Helen Humphreys
Daniel David Moses
Diane Schoemperlen
Merilyn Simonds
Carolyn Smart

Contents

The university art gallery exercises a privilege, indeed a mandate, of serving as a locus for experimentation, to challenge itself and its audiences to consider relationships with the art form. In contemporary art practice, the Agnes Etherington Art Centre has explored these relationships in a number of ways in recent exhibitions such as *Museopathy, Better Worlds,* and *Machine Life,* each in its own way embracing broad, even unexpected, definitions of artistic creation and its presence in the physical and ideological environments.

Telling Stories, Secret Lives is another such experiment. Here, curator Jan Allen has brought together a diverse—even incongruous—selection of recent work in an array of media from our permanent collection, and has posited its shared narrative purpose. To parse it, she has introduced a platform for a second layer of meanings by inviting an equal number of writers to muse and to create their own responsive texts, to investigate what she has called "combinatory aesthetics." For the viewer, and the readers of this catalogue, the result is a shared stage between production and reception, one that challenges us to consider that the conceptual and cognitive processes that inform creation are fluid, open, and ultimately transitory. To her, and to the senior artists and writers who collaborated in this exhibition, I offer my congratulations for shaping this productive encounter between the distinct languages of two art forms, and for creating this adventure in looking and reading.

On behalf of the Art Centre, I offer thanks to the Ontario Arts Council and the Canada Council for the Arts, whose programming grants have supported this project. I also acknowledge the crucial contributions of the Canada Council for the Arts Acquisition Assistance Program, the Chancellor Richardson Memorial Fund at Queen's University, and the Canada Council Art Bank, whose sustained support has strengthened our contemporary collection over the years with important acquisitions, including many of the works in this exhibition.

Janet M. Brooke

Director

Inspired by a recent upsurge in the use of story telling in contemporary art, the Art Centre invited seven of Kingston's finest writers to produce short texts in response to installation and sculptural works in our collection. The resulting stories and poems by Jill Battson, Steven Heighton, Helen Humphreys, Daniel David Moses, Diane Schoemperlen, Merilyn Simonds, and Carolyn Smart, presented here, extend the web of imaginative possibilities embedded in each piece. Art critical discourses, enthralled as they have been with conceptualism in recent years, have tended to suppress the story lines—implicit or explicit—in many works of art; but, today, the use of compelling narrative motive in art is, once more, in the foreground of art practices. This show offers a reconsideration of installation and sculptural works that takes into account their narrative potential by extending and making tangible the trajectories they embody.

Many of the large-scale pieces in this exhibition entered the Art Centre's collection recently, and have not previously been shown in Kingston. Spanning three galleries, this experimental exhibition presents works by major Canadian artists: Dorothy Cameron, Ian Carr-Harris, Robin Collyer, Vera Frenkel, Myfanwy MacLeod, Sandra Meigs, and Terry Pfliger.

This publication echoes the exhibition by presenting the inventive commissioned texts adjacent to images of the subject work. In the essay "Experiments in Combinatory Aesthetics" I respond in turn to the texts, considering: the distinct ways in which each has addressed the work of art, the nature of visual art and writing practices, and their capacity to generate reflective social space in culture.

A crucial third section of the publication consists of catalogue entries on each of the works of art. These summary texts, selected artists' statements, and biographical notes touch on the significance of the works of art within the mainstream of current art discourses. This material formed the basis of dossiers through which we introduced the subject works to the participating writers, but it should be noted that it was not made available to audiences during the run of the exhibition.

Many talented people made *Telling Stories, Secret Lives* a reality. I thank the artists for the amazing works that constitute the heart and first stimulus of this project. Enormous thanks are due to the participating writers: I'm grateful for their warm responses to the invitation to be a part of this project, and most of all for their superb texts. In the course of preparing *Telling Stories, Secret Lives*, I have had the benefit of able assistants. Initial research dossiers were prepared by the energetic and astute Meaghan Lowe. Steven Matijcio provided key support in development of the project, and sensitively crafted the catalogue entries published herein. Tabitha Minns provided further assistance in preparation of the publication. Among my Art Centre colleagues, Pat Sullivan and Annabel Hanson deserve accolades for their extraordinary work in support of this exhibition and the palette of interpretive events that surrounded it. Special thanks to Barbara Klempan and Dave Turnbull for their vital work on the restoration of *The Lost Goddess*. Lastly, I must single out writer Carolyn Smart, whose early encouragement and advice were key to the successful realization of the project: I thank her for her unstinting generosity.

Jan Allen
Curator of Contemporary Art

Telling Stories, Secret Lives

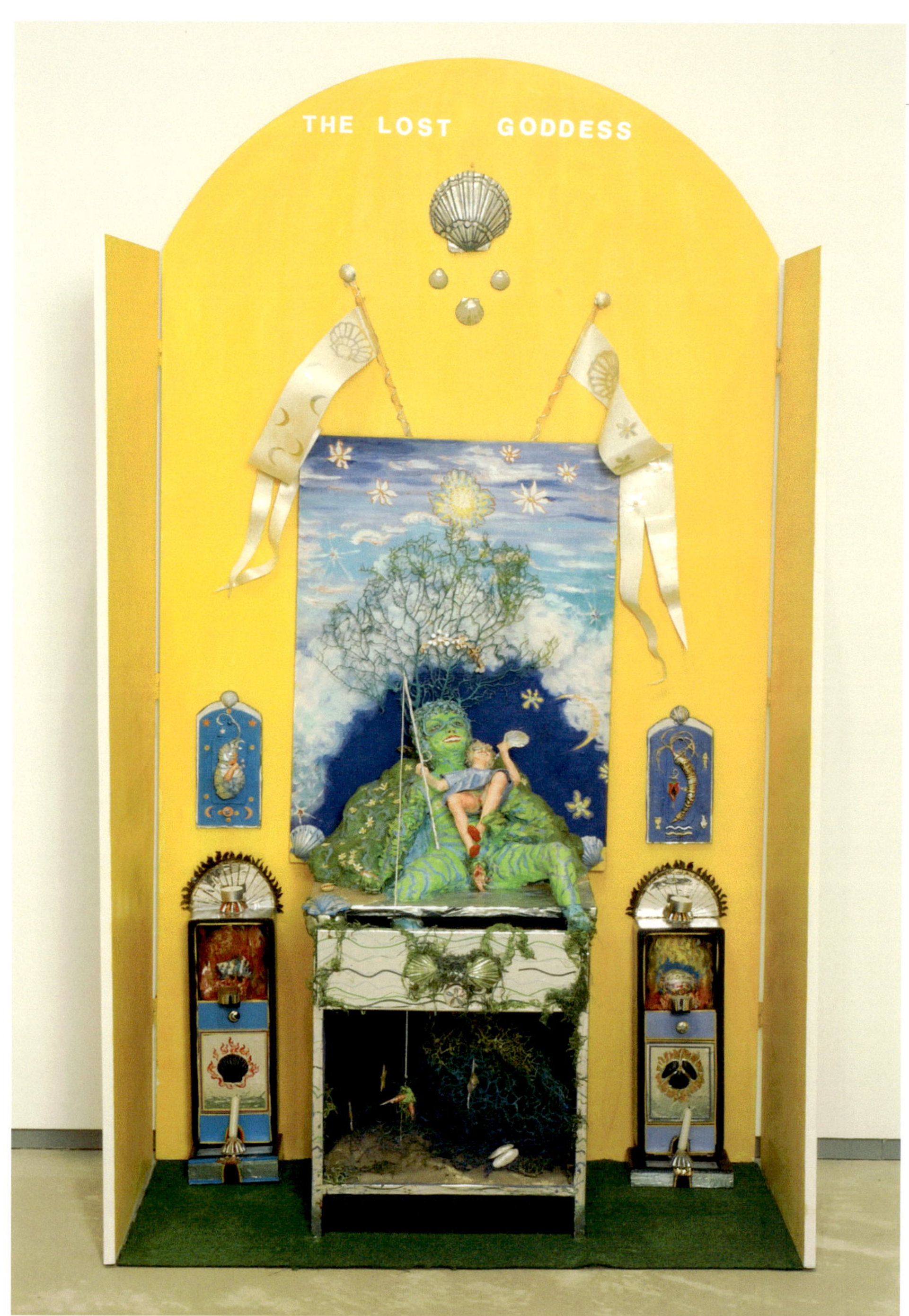

1.6

Fishy Business
Jill Battson

giving birth to the divine

I am of the earth, sky, ocean
the universe crowns my head, a magnificat of stars
ocean's soft wetness warms my feet
I am leaves, grass, flowers
my body runs with rivers and streams
a canyon between foothills of my belly gapes red

Exhausted from my earthly incarnation
as the mother of christ
I lay serene through millennia
forgotten, in paganized exile as
wars, torture, christianity, patriarchy
punish my body in the name of the saviour
my fishy-boy mistake with the rough and perforated palms

Gestation of two thousand years
to counter with a feminine divinity
I labour through plagues, earthquakes,
shifting tectonic plates of tsunamis
blossoms open like time-lapses over my mantle of boulders
I bear down in the screaming thunder of storms
and snapping corals of the tranquil depths

From within comes a fish so naked
she dons a silver grey armour to survive
curled against history, she wears the
beady-eyed mask of religion
I give a last gasp of fecundity to right wrongs
she is the child of my nature, born to harmonize
her naked vulnerability shielded against mankind.

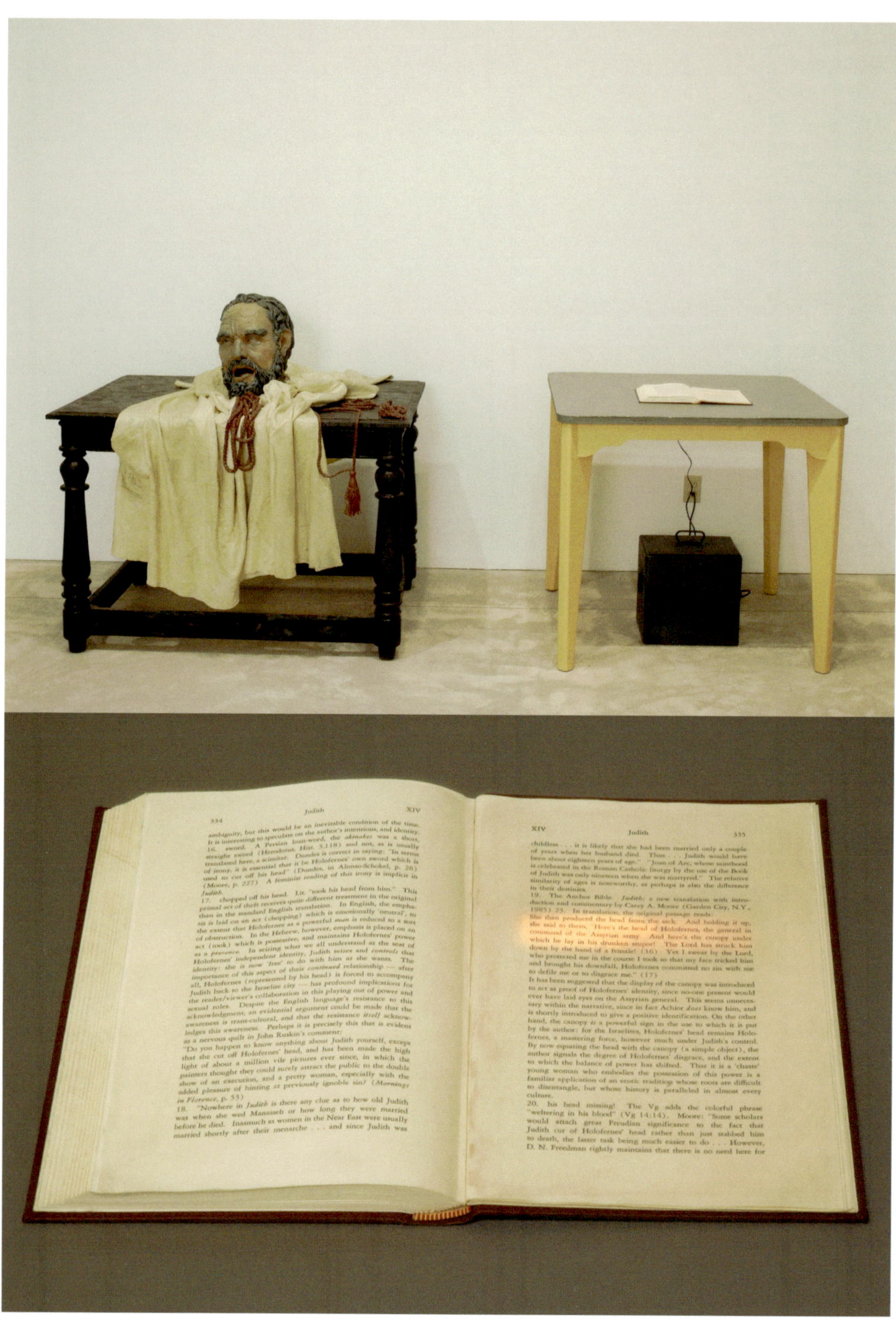

Judith   XIV
334
ambiguity, but this would be an inevitable condition of the time.
It is interesting to speculate on the author's intentions, and identity.
16.   sword.   A Persian loan-word, the akinakes was a short,
straight sword (Herodotus, Hist. 5.118) and not, as is usually
translated here, a scimitar.   Dundes is correct in saying: "In terms
of irony, it is essential that it be Holofernes' own sword which is
used to cut off his head" (Dundes, in Alonso-Schokel, p. 28)
(Moore, p. 227)   A feminist reading of this irony is implicit in
Judith.
17.   chopped off his head.   Lit. "took his head from him."   This
primal act of theft receives quite different treatment in the original
than in the standard English translation.   In English, the emphasis is laid on an act (chopping) which is emotionally 'neutral', to
the extent that Holofernes as a powerful man is reduced to a sort
of obstruction.   In the Hebrew, however, emphasis is placed on an
act (took) which is possessive, and maintains Holofernes' power
as a presence.   In seizing what we all understand as the seat of
Holofernes' independent identity, Judith seizes and controls that
identity: she is now 'free' to do with him as she wants.   The
importance of this aspect of their continued relationship — after
all, Holofernes (represented by his head) is forced to accompany
Judith back to the Israelite city — has profound implications for
the reader/viewer's collaboration in this playing out of power and
sexual roles.   Despite the English language's resistance to this
acknowledgment, an evidential argument could be made that the
awareness is trans-cultural, and that the resistance itself acknowledges this awareness.   Perhaps it is precisely this that is evident
as a nervous quilt in John Ruskin's comment:
"Do you happen to know anything about Judith yourself, except
that she cut off Holofernes' head, and has been made the high
light of about a million vile pictures ever since, in which the
painters thought they could surely attract the public to the double
show of an execution, and a pretty woman, especially with the
added pleasure of hinting at previously ignoble sin? (Mornings
in Florence, p. 53)
18.   "Nowhere in Judith is there any clue as to how old Judith
was when she wed Manasseh or how long they were married
before he died.   Inasmuch as women in the Near East were usually
married shortly after their menarche . . . and since Judith was

XIV   Judith   335
childless . . . it is likely that she had been married only a couple
of years when her husband died.   Thus . . . Judith would have
been about eighteen years of age."   "Joan of Arc, whose sainthood
is celebrated in the Roman Catholic liturgy by the use of the Book
of Judith was only nineteen when she was martyred."   The relative
similarity of ages is noteworthy, as perhaps is also the difference
in their destinies.
19.   The Anchor Bible.   Judith: a new translation with introduction and commentary by Carey A. Moore (Garden City, N.Y.,
1985) 23.   In translation, the original passage reads:
She then produced the head from the sack.   And holding it up,
she said to them, 'Here's the head of Holofernes, the general in
command of the Assyrian army.   And here's the canopy under
which he lay in his drunken stupor!   The Lord has struck him
down by the hand of a female!   (16)   Yet I swear by the Lord,
who protected me in the course I took so that my face tricked him
and brought his downfall, Holofernes committed no sin with me
to defile me or to disgrace me." (17)
It has been suggested that the display of the canopy was introduced
to act as proof of Holofernes' identity, since no-one present would
ever have laid eyes on the Assyrian general.   This seems unneces-
sary within the narrative, since in fact Achior does know him, and
is shortly introduced to give a positive identification. On the other
hand, the canopy is a powerful sign in the use to which it is put
by the author: for the Israelites, Holofernes' head remains Holofernes, a mastering force, however much under Judith's control.
By now equating the head with the canopy (a simple object), the
author signals the degree of Holofernes' disgrace, and the extent
to which the balance of power has shifted.   That it is a 'chaste'
young woman who embodies the possession of this power is a
familiar application of an erotic tradition whose roots are difficult
to disentangle, but whose history is paralleled in almost every
culture.
20.   his head missing!   The Vg adds the colorful phrase
"weltering in his blood" (Vg 14:14).   Moore: "Some scholars
would attach great Freudian significance to the fact that
Judith cut of Holofernes' head rather than just stabbed him
to death, the latter task being much easier to do . . . However,
D. N. Freedman rightly maintains that there is no need here for

1.8

Ian Carr-Harris (b. 1941, Victoria, British Columbia)
*The Anchor Bible, "Judith"; A New Translation with Introduction and Commentary
by Carey A. Moore (Garden City, N.Y., 1985), 23.*
1988

Testament
Merilyn Simonds

And she struck his neck twice with all her might, and severed his head from his body. Then she tumbled his body off the bed and pulled down the canopy from the posts; after a moment[†] she went out, and gave Holofernes' head to her maid, who placed it in her food bag.

The Book of Judith 13: 8–10

from *The Apocrypha*

O Lord God! Look upon the work of my hands!

The head rolled, coming to rest against a hillock of rumpled fabric, face upright among the folds. Even then, it was not still. Eyelids and lips contorted in irregular, rhythmic spasms until after five seconds, maybe six, the contractions ceased and the lids half-closed as if overcome by sleep, only the white of conjunctiva visible.

Holofernes!

Slowly the eyelids lifted, pupils tracking toward the sound. Through a ruddy mist, he saw her, heard her heaving breath, felt it hot across his brow. *What have you done, woman?* His voice to his own ears ripe with command, though his lips were fixed, a sluggish howl.

Holofernes! See the beauty of the countenance that has brought the enemy of my people low.

Again he strained against the weight of flesh that hooded his eyes, and there it was, his body at a distance, though he lunged his thighs toward her, grasped at the sword she held flush to her breast. *All the world I have conquered, and this is how it ends?*

Once more he raised his eyelids, fastened one faintly living eye on hers. *Why do you linger then? Hoist this head upon your parapet. This whorl of flesh. Let ravens ream out these eyes, worms devour what gives shape to these bones, for I am immortal. My name will endure, as will yours, though not as a testament to your beauty or your cunning, your unnatural courage. From this moment, you live through me. So pick up my head, hold it high in your hands. We are one.*

† In 1905, Dr Beaurieux observed closely the head of a criminal immediately after decapitation by guillotine. Periodically, he called out the man's name. The eyes opened and fixed on his, the gaze more penetrating each time, until at last there was no response. "The whole thing," Beaurieux wrote, "lasted twenty-five to thirty seconds."

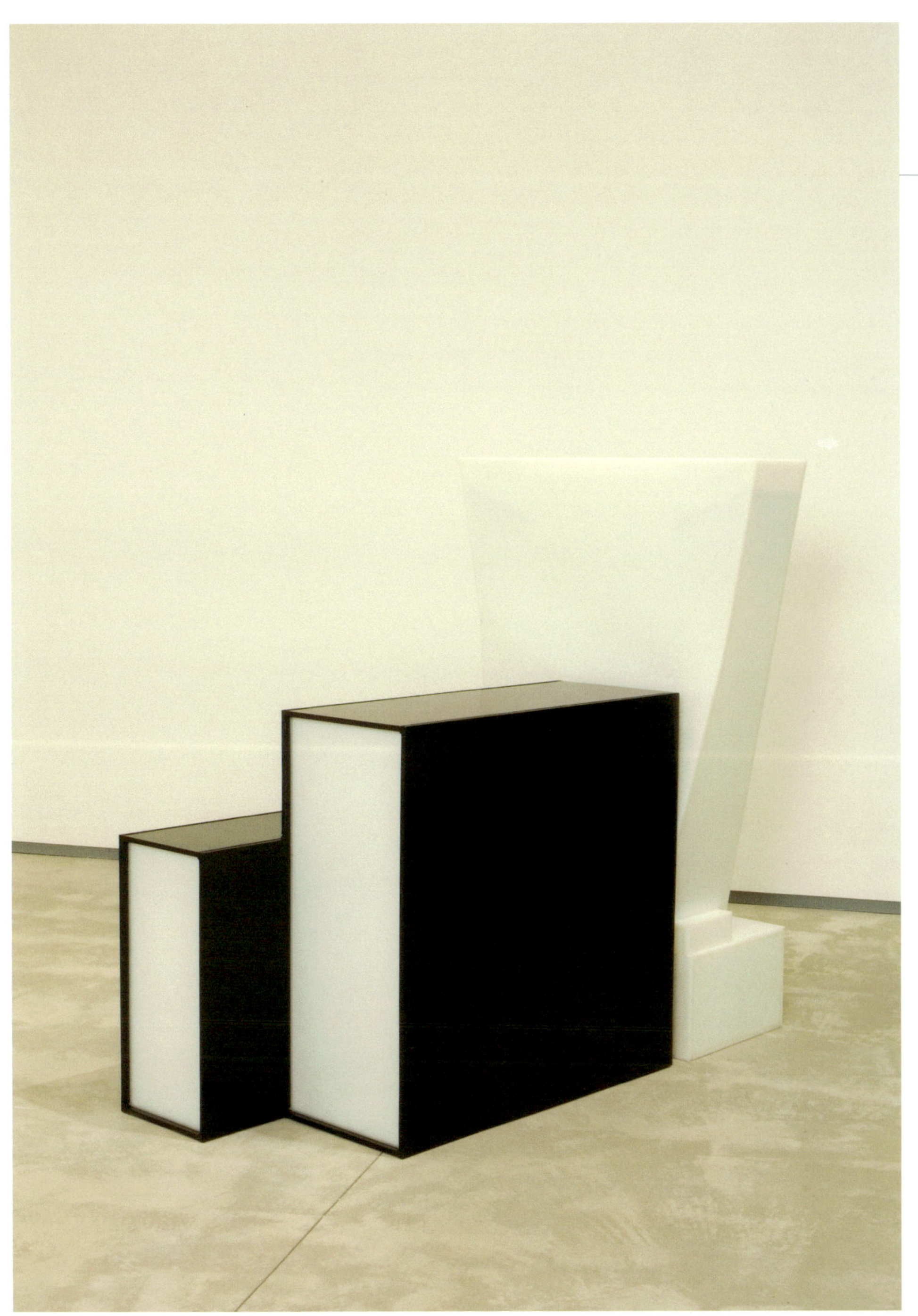

Big Noise
Daniel David Moses

An altar, you guess, one that need never know
       ceremony. Yes, something this small, one
could hide in the house, conduct worship at
      in secret or in private. *The surfaces are blanks, erased pages,*
          censored texts. Whatever gods or holy
        ghosts first inspired the faithful have faded
         away, ashamed, or been outlawed. And something

so simplified should serve a faith with no
      need of pomp or witnesses, a belief
in ideas, yourself and your senses. *So all*

        one's left to worship has no name, can only
         be described as black and white, left or
       right, with right and sometimes oblique and some
         few other angles too, as down and up.
    And liturgies then would gasp out their last

supplications, mutter nostalgically
      praising hymns. When that silence comes to pass,
no style of the spiritual will call
      on you to sacrifice or be the goat.

        How simple rectilinear makes things!
         What comfort comes from the world abstracted.
        Suddenly quod erat demonstrandum
         is forever and forever, amen.

And whatever uses there were for moon
        light or the starred evening, forget them.
These receptacles, despite their surface
        resemblances, gather neither. Forget

about curves and fractals, about bones and
        veins and the wrinkling, too, of skin. Forget
about the ringing of dried wood and belled
        metal, about the old and young singing.

This is as close to perfection as you
        would ever want to get, a few steps back
from that edge. *Quod erat demonstrandum,*
        yes, forever and forever, amen.

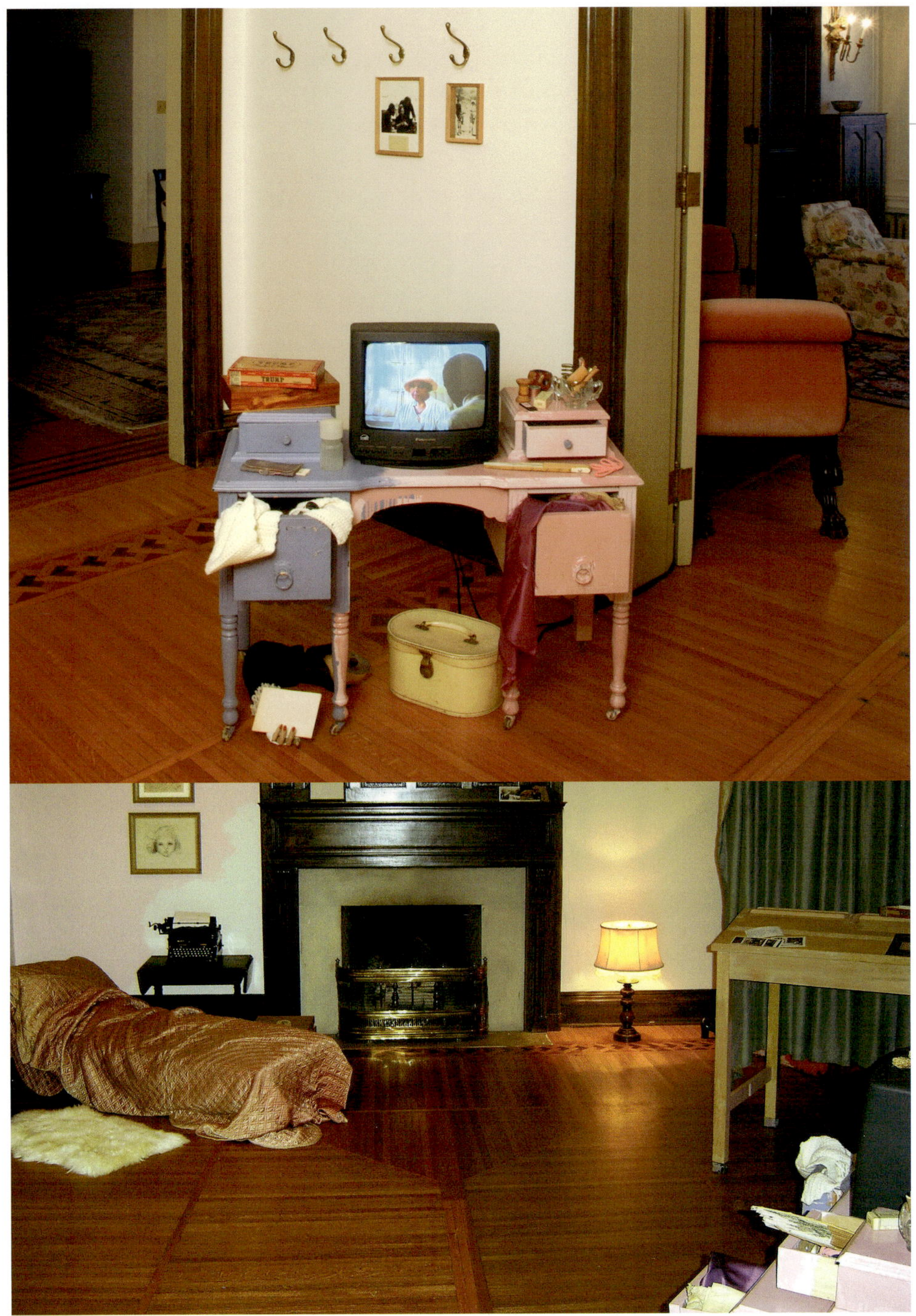

Each room we enter is a museum.
The beads, the dress, this desiccated rose —
evidence of how we live.
But nothing to tell us who we are.

No word can fasten what is fugitive
to a story we can trust.
No phrase or gesture can be emptied.
No witness is reliable.

There is only the shifting breath of blood
in our bodies to believe in.
Only that, and our small fidelities
to this earth and one another.

Every life is a secret life.
Nothing holds its truth for long enough.

Helen Humphreys

< detail views

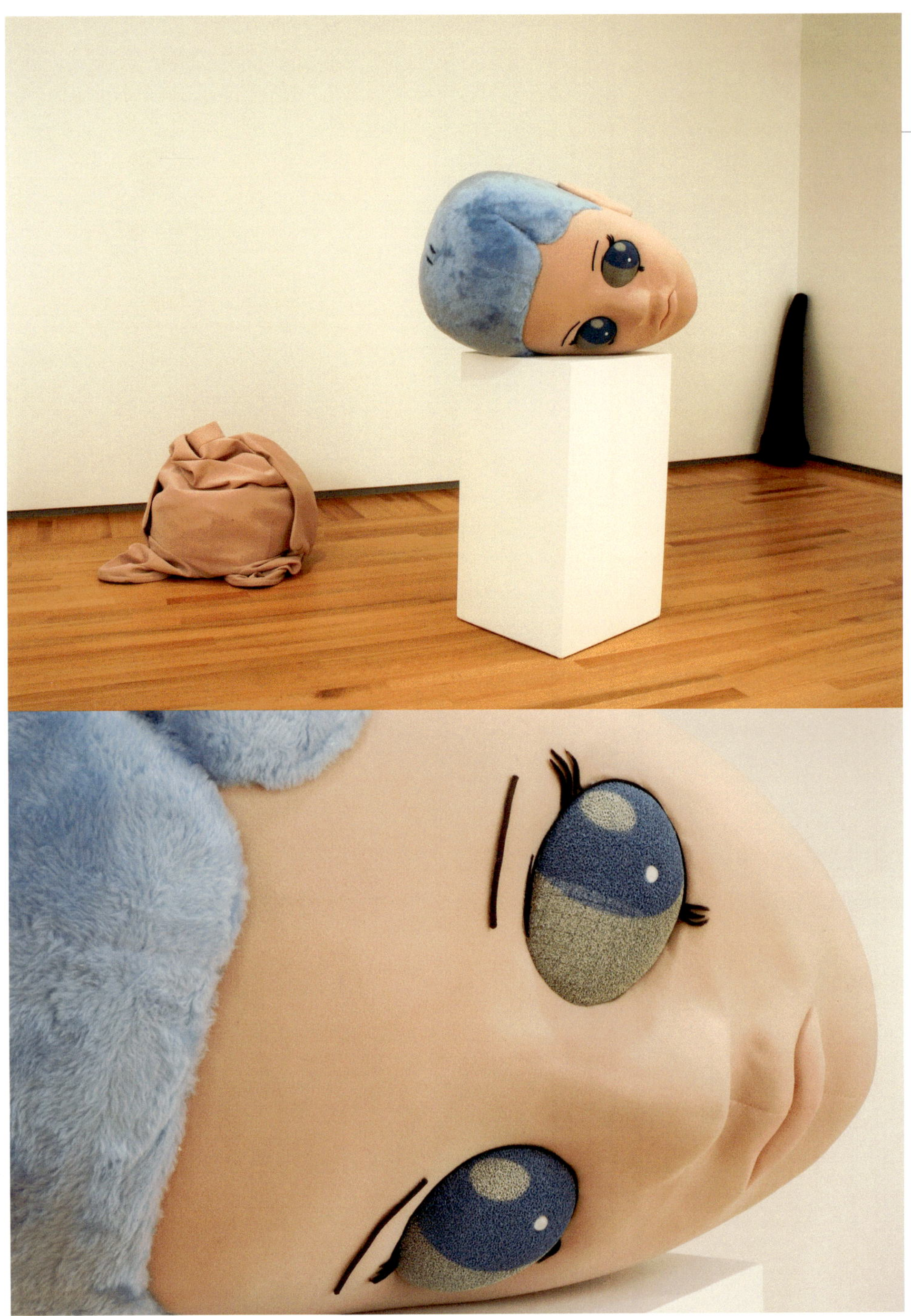

1.16

The Mascot
Steven Heighton

The installation / a comic strip head on its side on a white plinth /
deflated small pink body clumped on the floor like a sloughed or flayed skin /
in the corner a dark Flintstone cudgel propped against the wall /

I am alone in this cartoon,

                         take my history: fable
of every-mascot, everyman, woman, adrift
in the thin atmosphere on this plinth, high as that famously
hallucinating saint perched decades on a pillar
in old Syria, like a magpie—a vulture
of his own slow decay,
his mortification—
and what do we have against the body anyhow?

My story: cartoon head on a pedestal, where once
were epic busts, limestone, marble, Socrates or Sappho
or that archaic torso of Apollo, the one in Rilke's sonnet
who jolts and cajoles you to LIVE
the altered life. One steeped
in love and belief.

                    I almost don't believe
that that was ever possible, seems so long and
How shall we sing? in such a desert. (I know
a desert when I'm in one.) Or space—far between the comfy
caravanserais of galaxies, systems, how I miss the home planet,
my body. It lies remote below, sloughed and shucked
like a superhero suit, though pink, not blue,
with smog and assorted
nautical toxins.

Start the telling in cavelit millennia, eras of flint of cudgel of
coughing soot and no escape from the palpably
dying flesh, the trembling in pelts, nursing burns, wolfing
other flesh raw—but also starting to outline in ochre and ashes
those first surging, sacred beasts, there beside the living
shadows of hands—starting to petal the husks of the dead,
in their permafrost graves, with gentian, rue
and bluebells.
        Our dead.
            Ice-sheets long as the Tigris withdrew, blue,
cold-blooded behemoths leery of our growing fires/
light/language/etchings—as if these miracles decreed their retreat!
In the thawing vales, first furrows appeared, harvests. First towns.
First cities. First comforts! Apparently life was to be more
than a brute bout with hypothermia and big
diligent predators.
        In our cavewall cartoons
our heads had been mere nubs—puny afterthoughts—our physiques
thick and big, wishfully well-fed. Now heads were growing
to proportion. Already there were: cuneiform scribes, accountants, astronomers, spies,
touts, troubadours, personal trainers, tort lawyers, stand up comics in jingling hats,
sculptors who would gouge (we're in Greece now) marble busts
with eyes blank as Modigliani's, or Rilke's Apollo's
visionary nipples—Yes because the whole person
was what saw, with body/mind still welded,
saw and thought and conceived——
        All those generations
our sensed enterprise was somehow to draw our being
into balance, muscled hunter and pensive angel/amorous phantom.
Eliot thought we'd arrived once, in Donne, Shakespeare, those few
thinking their feelings and feeling their thought.
Not quite, no not nearly, though we were getting somewhere.
But the head grew onward, with the tumorous ego
(which, now I think of it, is just fear, old fears
of the dying beast we seem to haul around
like a lumbersome graft—that ancient Judas,
our animal. A death jungled inside us . . .).

But we had ways now, a little learning, ambition, technology,
the full arsenal of immortality. We had Nature
pinned down. And the head kept swelling, packed
with a madness of data / metastatic taxonomies /
the hoarder's drive to confiscate, control. The whole
Puritan imperative.
                Lastly Nature with its inconvenient
demands is banished to mechanical gyms. Maintained
with occasional Day-timer sex. Is fully authentic
& collectible. May be hanged in the closet
till required, then removed, dusted off like the curious
vestige of a primitive rite. . . .

I should have danced more and drawn fewer blueprints.

Here I am / perfected emblem / effigy of the age /
on my column surfing my own brainwaves like
someone adrift in a video game. Hair cyan-blue, huge
spongiform eyes, head sidewise staring upward, in
some concern, apparently, alone in this cartoon and
missing earth, my own flesh, the coursing
brooks of my blood, all lost with "the silver
reaches of the estuary"——

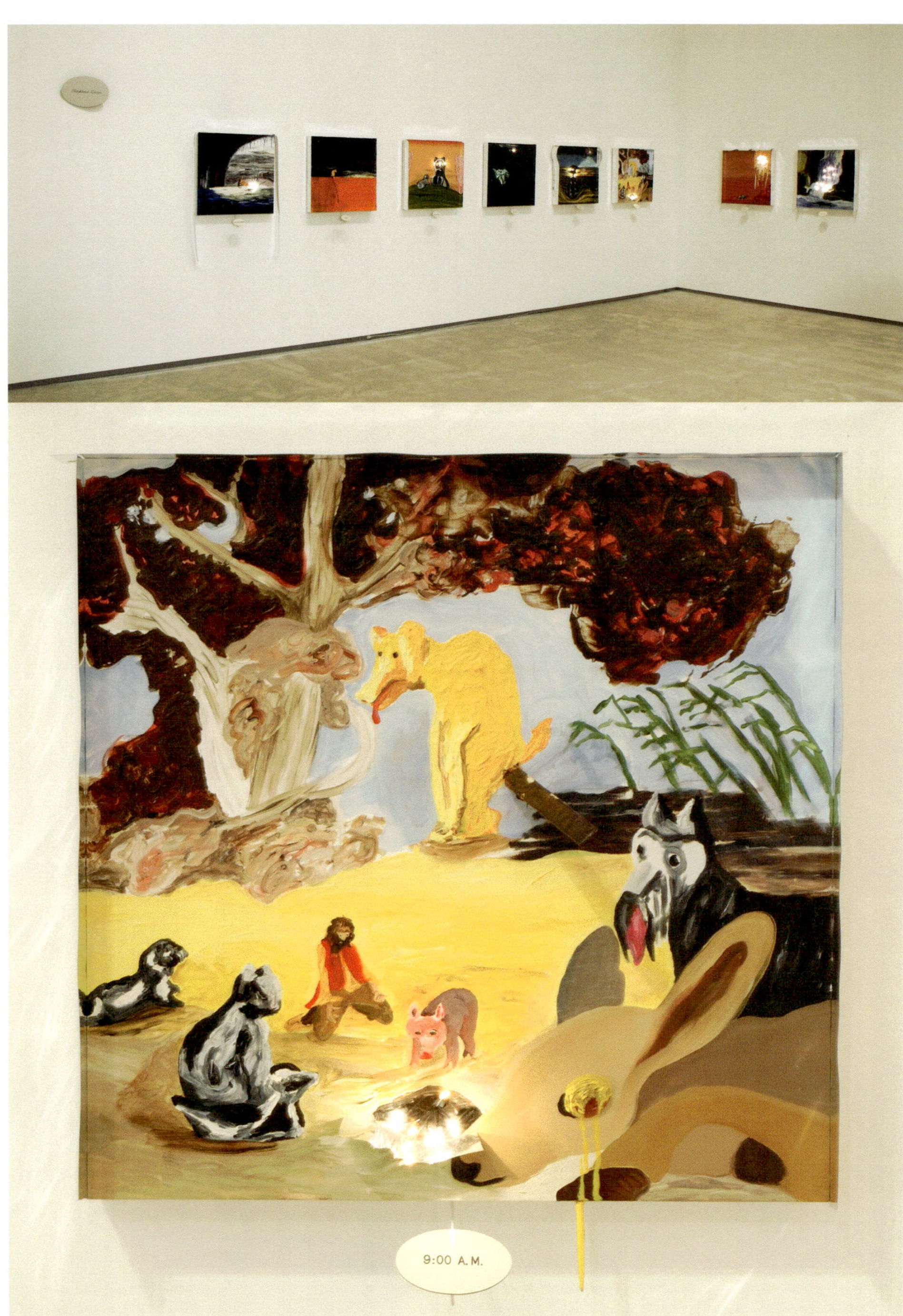

9:00 A.M.

Sandra Meigs (b. 1963, Baltimore, Maryland)
Reckless Days
1997

When I was young
Carolyn Smart

When I was young, I was in the care of two women. Their names were Jane and Grace. Jane was very urbane, very breezy, very lipsticked. She never lifted a duster in her life. Grace was soft; she was proper and colourless. She told me Jane was a saint. Jane drank dry martinis straight up with a twist. Grace had a single sweet sherry before lunch on Sundays.

Grace told me to sit on my potty and give it a good try. So I'd sit and sit and sit and imagine what was living in my body, in the little cave of my body, warm and comfortable and dry, and what wanted to come out. After a while I'd drift back into the nursery and Grace would say "Did you try?" and I would say that if she looked in my potty, she would see some try.

Jane was hazy about bodily functions but she was pretty sharp about language. She didn't like rudeness. She hit me across the face in a public elevator. Men were watching, or maybe it was only one man.

The first thing I stole was a Barbie head. It fit perfectly inside of my closed fist. Jane asked me how I managed to get another head for my Barbie and I said that my best friend's mother had driven by in her blue convertible and had pulled over to the side of the road and said "I knew you would want this: here it is." My best friend's mother looked like Grace Kelly and she used to sing in an off-key sort of way and most people would ignore it but I liked it, it made me happy. Jane said I had to take that Barbie head right back to where I stole it. God would be watching, she said. And how did I think I could get away with something like that, anyway? Who did I think I was?

That summer I almost drowned. I was swimming with two girls. One had very broad shoulders and hunched her body over. She was hiding her chests, Grace said. The big girl had a younger sister who jumped around a lot. They were like a gorilla and a gorilla's tiny friend. The three of us tried pulling up the ropes that held the swimming raft in place. There were rocks weighing down the ropes and when I swam beneath the raft I could see the light of day above me and the deep green water, the sweet dark lake filled with flecks that sparked and bobbled like an invitation. When I dropped the rock the cord wrapped and twisted round my legs; it pulled me down. I looked up towards the bright surface of the water, the innocent legs of girls kicking around on a warm afternoon, and I was enthralled.

One can only imagine what might happen next. One can only try.

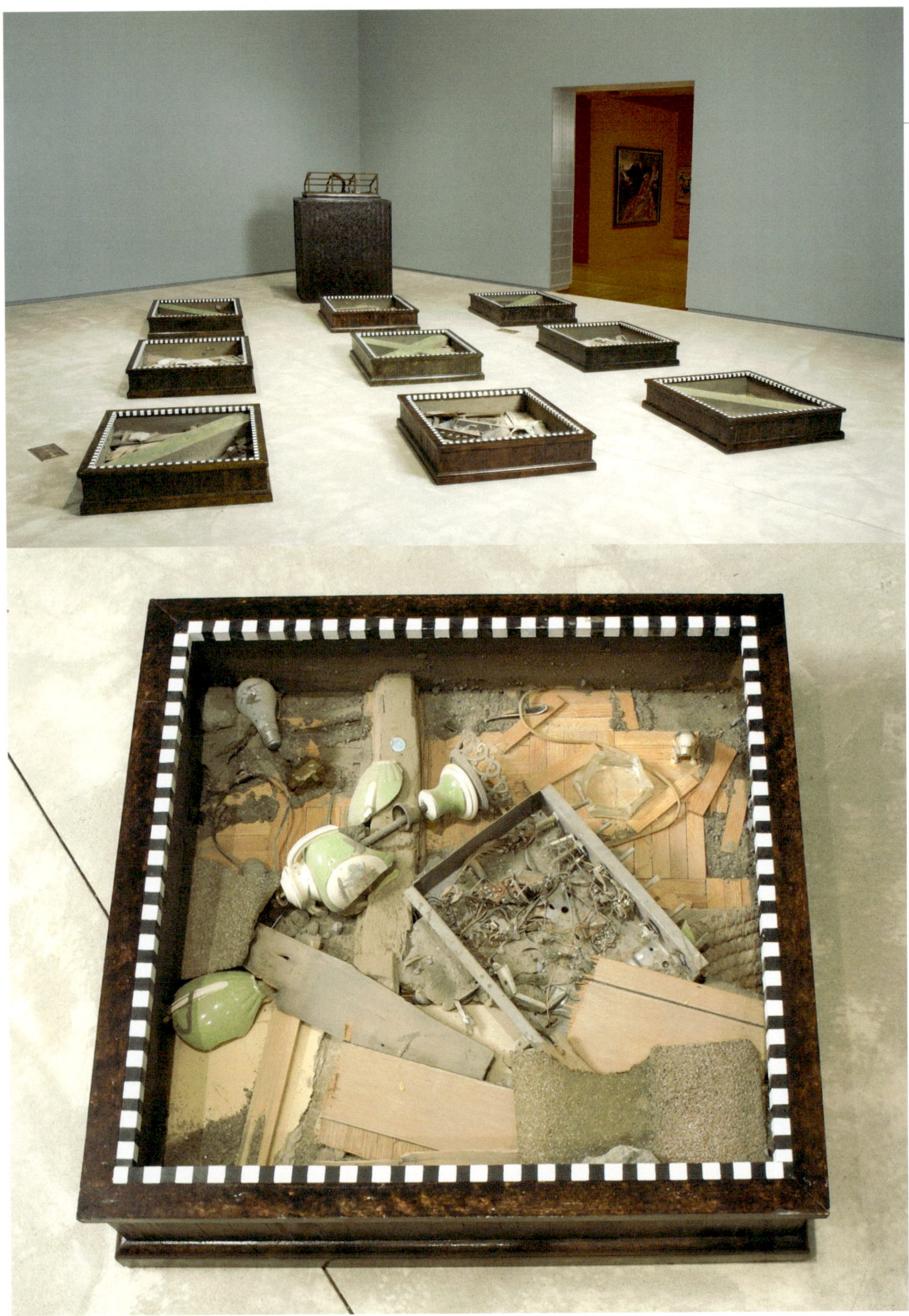

1.22

Evolution is but a Long and Complicated Wish … or, it's about Time!
by Terry Pfliger
Diane Schoemperlen

Charles Darwin said: *The whole history of the world, as at present known, although of a length quite incomprehensible to us, will hereafter be recognised as a mere fragment of time, compared with the ages which have elapsed since the first creature, the progenitor of innumerable extinct and living descendants, was created.*

1.   Two ceramic panthers bide their time in the china cabinet, leashed together with a tiny gold chain. Plastic ferns are popular: all good families have them. At school, smart children are learning about archaeology and ambition.

2.   Women spend hours talking on the phone, but nothing gets resolved. Men repaint their living rooms in the same cream colour they've always been. Three shingles are blown off the roof in a thunderstorm. A boy eats peaches from a plain white bowl.

3.   Men like to go golfing in white shoes. Women weigh themselves obsessively. Young girls sleep restlessly in small beds crowded with stuffed animals. For eleven months of the year, the Christmas tree ornaments are kept in a box in the basement. At the beginning of December, they are set free.

4.   Some houses are filled with music, but others are not. Sometimes there is singing. No one knows how the globe got broken. Or at least, no one will admit to breaking the globe. The broken globe assumes the power of a bad omen. People begin to feel anxious.

5.   A child eats candies from a silver dish: hard candies wrapped in foil: raspberry, lemon, and orange. It rains every day for a week. Cookies are baked in the shape of dogs.

6.   A woman fries eggs for breakfast while wearing a gold chain around her neck. Later: the yolks ooze yellow across the blue plates. Later still: the chain is lost, sliding down the kitchen drain like a snake.

7.   Later: the broom handle is broken, the curtain rod falls down, a man loses his keys and has to wait outside his own house in the snow. He stamps his feet in the cold. All winter long, the citizens listen only to Baroque music.

8.   Later still: the green lamp is broken, the stereo is smashed, all the lightbulbs have burned out at once. Some people think the world is ending, one piece at a time.

9.   A woman puts out her cigarette in a small green glass ashtray and then she turns out the lights and locks the door. The dust settles over everything. No one seems to notice.

10.   Someday a boat will crash into the pier. There will be screaming. There will be smoke. There will be injuries but no deaths. This will be the only event of the day that makes the evening news. All the rest will be forgotten.

Life goes on.

Time goes by.

Despite expectations and omens to the contrary, the world does not end after all.

Charles Darwin said: *There is grandeur in this view of life, with its several powers, having been originally breathed into a few forms or into one; and that, whilst this planet has gone cycling on according to the fixed law of gravity, from so simple a beginning endless forms most beautiful and wonderful have been, and are being, evolved.*

Contents

Telling Stories, Secret Lives

Catalogue and Artists' Biographical Notes

Steven Matijcio

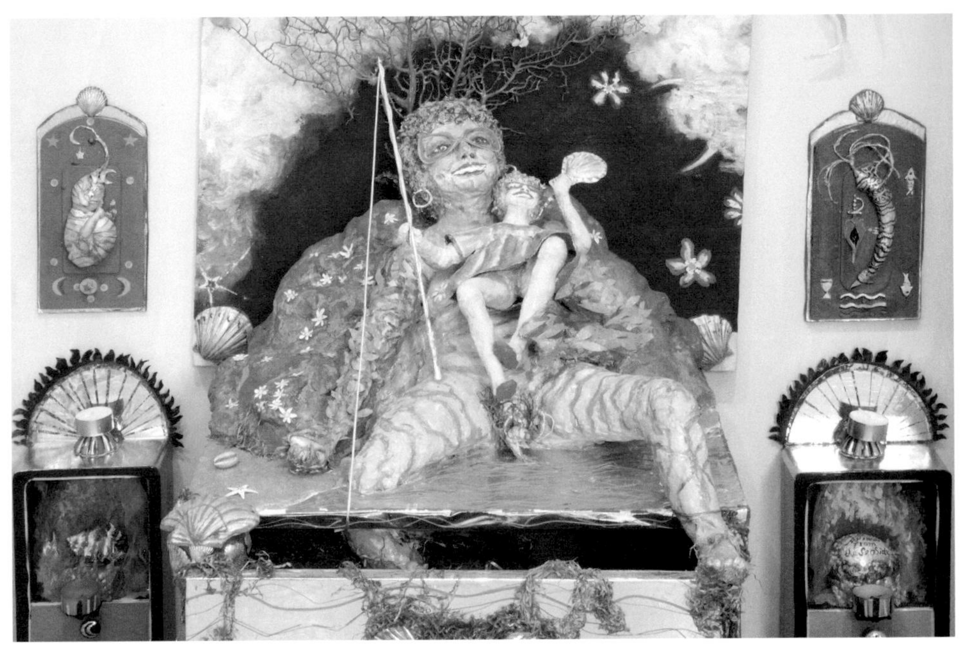

Dorothy Cameron (1924–2000, Toronto)

The Lost Goddess

1980

Mixed media

Three-part folding panel: 197 x 101 cm

Free-standing elements: 88 x 42 x 52 cm

Collection of Agnes Etherington Art Centre

Donated by a friend, in loving memory of the remarkable gallerist and artist, Dorothy Cameron, 2003

46-036

Described as "the miraculous babies of my post-menopausal years," Dorothy Cameron's sculptural work draws upon her recollections of life, family, sexuality, and death. *The Lost Goddess* was one of the first in this collection, inspired by the theories of famed psychoanalyst Carl Jung and Cameron's own quest for self-discovery. Made just two years after she lost all sight in her right eye, this work was inspired by a dream that the artist vividly recounts in an accompanying statement. It is mounted upon a metal cabinet, framed by a three-part screen, and constructed from self-hardening modelling compounds, papier mâché, paint,

and a collection of traditionally feminine objects like dolls, ribbons, candles, and pearls. What ensues is highly ornamental but grounded by Cameron's self-professed employment of it as a tool for self-analysis rather than as a purely aesthetic object.

In the account of her dream, Cameron recalls the labour of an ancient goddess of ocean, earth, and sky—her legs spread as she emerges from the land and births a small shrimp. The artist explains that this Goddess is a future version of the Virgin Mary, and her "shrimp-child" represents the feminine counterpart of the Christ Child (symbolized by the fish). The shrimp is fitting to this feminine figure because this divine newborn shares what Cameron considers the fate of all earthly women: needing armour to protect its naked vulnerability.

Extending the allegory a step further, another woman lays on the lap of the goddess —her legs similarly spread as she handles a fishing rod in hopes of hooking a shrimp-child. Both goddess and earthly subject are obvious self-portraits of the artist—sharing the same hairstyle and eyeglasses—but Cameron coyly concludes, "If woman and Goddess appear to resemble each other, it is because they both reflect the restored radiance of female identity and self-worth."

Artist's Statement

This piece was based on a dream, which I will try to interpret:

The ancient Goddess of Ocean, Earth, and Sky is giving birth. With her head crowned in stars, her feet in the sea, her arms covered in leaves, her legs running with blue streams, her vagina like a red slit in a green hill, the Great Goddess is bringing forth ... a *shrimp*.

Two thousand years ago, as Mary, she gave birth to the Christ child, that divine *male* aspect of her being whose symbol was the fish.

Today she is giving birth to the long-lost child of her own nature, her *feminine* self, symbolized in this little shrimp ... a fish so naked, so vulnerable, it must wear armour as its swaddling bands in order to survive. Seated on the Divine Lap, a diminutive woman with a fishing rod is busily hooking her own shrimp. If woman

and Goddess appear to resemble each other, it is because they both reflect the restored radiance of female identity and self-worth.

Dorothy Cameron

Biography

Dorothy Cameron was born in Toronto and raised in Kirkland Lake, Ontario, with her sister Anna. She achieved a BA in English at the University of Toronto in the late 1940s, followed by studies in contemporary art at the ICA in Boston (under the auspices of Harvard University). She opened the Here and Now Gallery in 1959. This eventually became the Dorothy Cameron Gallery (in 1962), functioning as a platform for the promotion of contemporary Canadian sculpture and artists such as Rita Letendre, Richard Turner, and Harold Town. Cameron established a strong reputation as an art dealer and is credited with developing the Toronto art scene in the 1960s, but was forced to shut down operations in 1965 after being convicted of exhibiting obscene material in the exhibition *Eros '65*. She fought the charges all the way to the Supreme Court of Canada, but ultimately lost the case in a landmark ruling that sparked much controversy on the subject of art and censorship.

Cameron went on to write, lecture, serve as a jury member on the Canada Council, and organize the major exhibition/festival *Sculpture '67* at the plaza of Toronto City Hall. In 1970 she married painter Ronald Bloore. Between 1978 and 1980, she lost sight in her right eye. This loss, surprisingly, launched her career as an artist as she engaged in a sculptural project of Jungian-inspired self-portraiture that would continue into the 1990s. These works were exhibited at the Lonsdale Gallery, as well as the Art Gallery of Hamilton and the Robert McLaughlin Gallery in Oshawa. After being diagnosed with pneumonia in December of 2000, Cameron passed away at the age of 75.

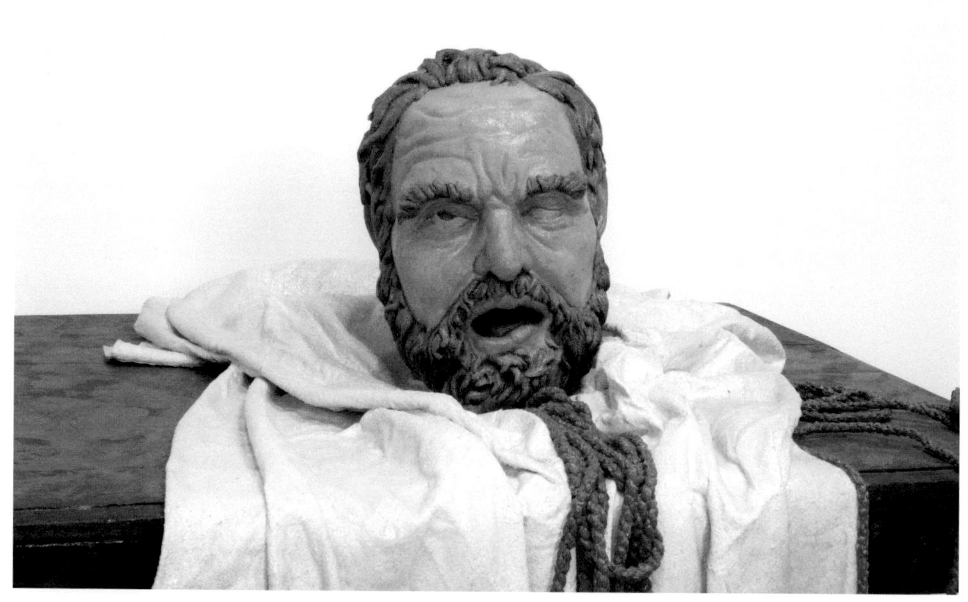

Ian Carr-Harris (b. 1941, Victoria, British Columbia)
The Anchor Bible, "Judith"; A New Translation with Introduction and Commentary
by Carey A. Moore (Garden City, N.Y., 1985), 23.
1988
Mixed media
119.4 x 285.8 x 104.1 cm
Collection of Agnes Etherington Art Centre
Purchase, Chancellor Richardson Memorial Fund, 1993
36-020

This work is part of a series based on the idea of transformation over time, where an original text shifts as it passes through successive writers. *Judith* refers to the story of Judith and Holofernes as told in the Apocrypha (or "Anchor Bible")—a collection of pre-Christian tales not officially endorsed by the Church despite their broad-based popularity. In this story, the heroine Judith saves her native city of Bethlia by seducing and then decapitating the general of an invading Assyrian army, Holofernes, as he lay in a drunken stupor.

The dramatic violence of this tale inspired many paintings in the Baroque period and beyond, but in Carr-Harris' version the heroine is absent—even as the

products of her act rest upon two separate tables. On the left-hand table, a plaster cast of Holofernes' head leans on a rope and drapery that have been treated with acrylic gel to mimic the varnished surface of paintings.

This tableau is accompanied by a book on the right-hand table. The book is open to a page of footnotes in which one passage is backlit. The illuminated note briefly recounts Judith's act, but is mixed in with other footnotes and excerpts from contemporary feminist interpretations of the story rather than the Apocryphal context. As such, both table displays can be seen as incomplete parts in an ongoing project of representation spanning both art and literature.

Artist's Statement

The work is one of a series of three associated works shown at the Carmen Lamanna Gallery in October/November 1998. All three were predicated on an idea of discursive expansion—that an "original" idea, event, memory, or whatever finds itself reappearing (can be tracked) through a series of references, allusions, and suggestions on an infinite trajectory marked by continuous and discontinuous implications.

I should note that the concept of illumination or illustration was paramount in my mind (a concept I associated with reproduction technologies and discursivity) as a correlative to language and printed books or magazines. Consequently, the table with the head of Holofernes has been treated not as an object in the world (i.e. an archaeological artifact) but as a painting from the fifteenth or sixteenth century—a kind of "reversed" artifact (painting/object rather than object/painting). The surfaces of this object/painting therefore are brushed with gel to resemble a painting's surface, and if the result slides close to kitsch, this is because in kitsch we have exposed for us the processes by which we transfer one concept/practice into another—in other words, the very processes of discursivity that inform these works as a whole.

Ian Carr-Harris

Biography

Ian Carr-Harris was born in Victoria, British Columbia, and raised in Ottawa. He achieved a BA in History at Queen's University in 1963, followed by a Bachelor of Library Science in 1964 at the University of Toronto and an AOCA diploma from the Ontario College of Art in 1971. Carr-Harris has been Director of Library Services and Chair of both the Experimental Arts and the Sculpture/ Installation programs, as well as Acting Chair for the Criticism and Curatorial program, at the Ontario College of Art and Design, where he continues to teach courses in studio and theory. Since 1971, he has exhibited nationally and internationally, with his work included in the *Paris Biennale* (1975), the *Venice Biennale* (1984), *Documenta 8* (1987), the *Canadian Biennial* at the National Gallery (1989), the *Sydney Biennale* (1990), the *Montreal Biennale* (1998), and *Threshold* at the Power Plant, Toronto (1998). His active publication schedule includes reviews and articles for such journals as *Canadian Art*, *Parachute*, *Contemporary Magazine*, and *C Magazine*, as well as catalogue essays. He was a founding board member of A Space (1971) and of the Power Plant (1987), and has served on the Harbourfront board and the board of the Art Gallery of Ontario. Carr-Harris resides in Toronto and is represented by Susan Hobbs Gallery.

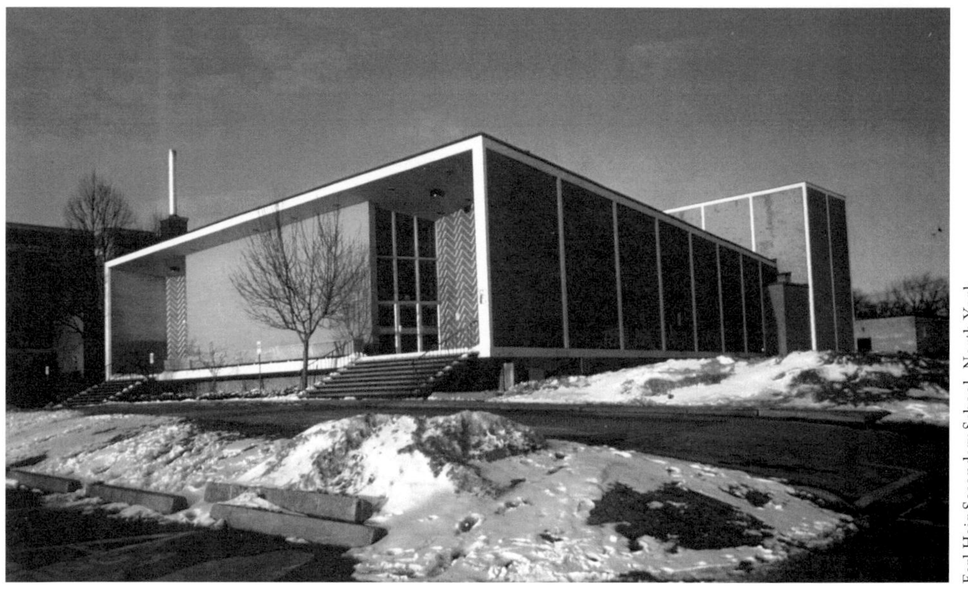

Robin Collyer (b. 1949, London, England)

Megaphone

1993

Polyethylene with metallic fabric

147.3 x 160 x 92.8 cm

Collection of Agnes Etherington Art Centre

Gift of the artist, 1998

41-017

Within Robin Collyer's larger body of work, *Megaphone* exemplifies a particular series where the artist uses a single material and the memory of architecture to create sculpture that includes aspects of himself. In this case, the two primary forms of *Megaphone* are inspired by structures that have personal relevance to the artist, and are built using a polyethylene associated with industrial sinks and vats.

The white form is based upon Collyer's high school auditorium (illustrated above), while the abutting black form is inspired by a 1954 insurance building whose scale and colour attracted the artist as he passed it on a Toronto street. The title of the piece refers to the shape and function of the auditorium, and the artist scaled both forms to his own bodily dimensions. However, any further autobiography is

complicated by his 180-degree reorientation of each building, and their construction out of the same standard material.

Many of Collyer's recent projects have drawn from his visual and physical responses to the urban environment, incorporating everything from billboards and vents to store shelves and media images. As he abstracts these forms by erasing their logos and introducing them in unusual contexts, one is left to question their historical legacy and the values they continue to transmit.

Artist's Statement

Simply speaking, *Megaphone* is made up of two distinct shapes that are small-scale facsimiles of two buildings.

One building is modelled after the shape of my high school auditorium (which is a classic megaphone shape), and the other is a small office building on St Clair Avenue (built in 1954). The material is polyethylene sheet in black and white.

This work was one of the first in an ongoing project that involves taking strategies in the construction of sculpture. The common elements in these sculptures are the use of (usually) one material for the complete work, and elements that are found or are a copy of some other structure. Other works in this group include *Tower, Kiosk, Desk, Application, Kennel,* and *The Most Violent Places.*

I wanted to produce sculpture with a minimum of aesthetic decision-making. So, in the case of *Megaphone*, instead of searching for interesting or beautiful shapes to incorporate into a 3-D composition, I chose two buildings; one I had a distinct relationship to, my high school, and the other, a modern building, attracted me by its scale and colour (the Anglo Canada Insurance Company building).

They were reproduced in the same unlikely material, made approximately my height, turned 180 degrees from the normal configuration, and butted up against each other.

There are, of course, a number of decisions made on my part. The conceptual framework is still my own, but I have produced sculpture in a more roundabout way, a way more interesting to me than, say, using composition as a tool to finalize the elements of a sculpture.

Ironically, it still remains an archetypal artwork in that it uses classic subjects, such as something from the past, a memory (high school), and something that attracted the artist by its beauty (the insurance company building).

Robin Collyer

Biography

Born in London, England, in 1949, Robin Collyer has lived and worked in Canada since 1957. Following studies at the Ontario College of Art in 1968, Collyer held his first solo exhibition at the Carmen Lamanna Gallery in Toronto. Since 1971, he has exhibited extensively in solo and group exhibitions across Canada, Europe, and the United States. Major exhibition venues include the Staatliche Kunsthalle, Baden-Baden (1992), the Barbican Art Gallery in London (1991), the Power Plant in Toronto (1990), and the Canadian Biennial of Contemporary Art at the National Gallery of Canada (1989). His work has been presented in solo exhibitions at the Musée de Beaux-Arts, Mulhouse, and Galerie Arlogos, Nantes (both 1992), Canada House, London (1989), Susan Hobbs Gallery, Toronto (1996), and Galerie Gilles Peyroulet, Paris (1993, 1995, 1998). Major surveys of his work have been presented at both the Agnes Etherington Art Centre (1982) and the Art Gallery of Ontario (1993). In addition, his work is held in numerous private and corporate collections, as well as in public collections in Canada and France.

Throughout his career, Collyer has demonstrated a consistent focus on the appropriation and abstraction of contemporary landscapes—moving between the media of photography and sculpture to conflate minimalist aesthetics and cultural critique. Issues such as the everyday effects of mass media and the social impact of urban sprawl are common themes of his work. The national significance of Collyer's work was confirmed with his representation of Canada at major international exhibitions like *Documenta 8* in Kassel (1987) and the 45th Venice Biennale (1993). In the latter, he exhibited a series of scaled down (anti) monuments that included *Megaphone*—speaking to the continuing resonance of modernist design in contemporary life. Collyer is currently based in Toronto and is represented by the Susan Hobbs Gallery.

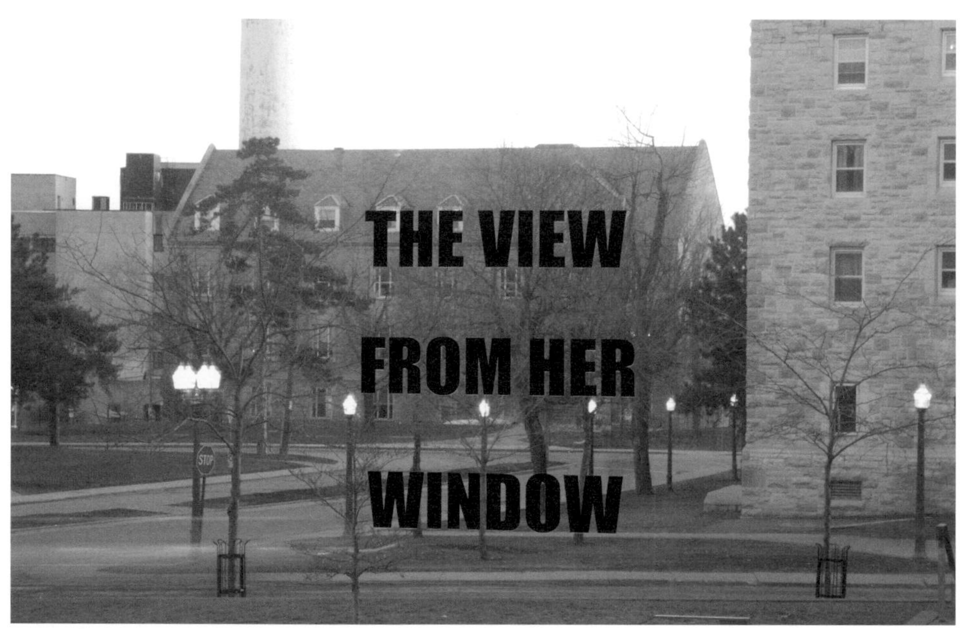

Vera Frenkel (b. 1938, Bratislava, Czechoslovakia)
Her Room in Paris
(The Secret Life of Cornelia Lumsden: A Remarkable Story, Part 1)
1979
Mixed-media installation, dimensions variable, installed: 18 square metres
Collection of Agnes Etherington Art Centre
Purchase, Chancellor Richardson Memorial Fund, 2004
46-043

Vera Frenkel's pioneering art practice has spanned multiple media to question the concept of truth and the ambiguity embedded in historical accounts. Moving along the borders between fact and fiction, she constructs worlds of multiple— often contradictory—layers. The Cornelia Lumsden project is a key example, described as "an extended work in progress using various combinations of media to reconstruct the life of a little known, but brilliant, Canadian novelist who lived in Paris between the wars."

Her Room in Paris is the first part in the intricate (but completely fictional) tale of Cornelia Lumsden, featuring a 60-minute video loop inside a room-like

installation. Lumsden is absent from her room, but the visitor is introduced to her through the furniture, clothes, and personal belongings littered through-out the half-painted chamber. Further introduction comes from testimonies of various acquaintances of the missing author, delivered via the video that plays on a monitor replacing the mirror atop Lumsden's vanity. Rather than clarifying the picture, however, these accounts only deepen the mystery.

The artist and her real-life colleague Tim Whiten play multiple parts in the video, drawing upon stereotypical roles of soap opera characters. Frenkel plays "The Friend," "The Rival," "The Expert," and "The CBC Reporter," and Whiten plays "The Lover" and "The Confidant." The stories they tell are full of inconsistency, and attention is drawn to the construction of both set and narrative as the fragmentary biography of Lumsden grows more complex.

Later instalments of the Cornelia Lumsden saga add to the uncertainty. In ... *And Now, The Truth (a Parenthesis)* (1981) a woman confronts Frenkel, claiming to be a relative of the real Cornelia Lumsden. In the computer-generated work *Lost Canadian* (1986), presented at Expo '86, issues of exile and mythmaking are further emphasized. And, in her most recent incarnation, Cornelia Lumsden appears in *The Institute*™*: Or, What We Do for Love* (1997 – ongoing), where she is identified as one of the first residents admitted into a fictional retirement home for artists.

Biography

Born in 1938 in Bratislava, Czechoslovakia, Vera Frenkel immigrated with her parents to Canada in 1950. After studies at McGill University, the Montreal Museum of Fine Arts, and the École des Beaux-Arts, she moved to Toronto where her first solo exhibitions took place, and she began to engage in a multi-disciplinary media arts practice. Her pioneering achievements include *String Games: Improvisations for Inter-City Video,* a work transmitted between two cities via Bell Canada teleconferencing facilities (1974). Since then, her installations, video-tapes, drawings, graphics, and performances have been presented in major festivals and galleries in Canada and elsewhere. In 1985, the National Gallery of Canada mounted a major survey of her video work, and in 1996 featured a reconstruction of her 6-channel *Documenta 9* installation *... from the Transit Bar.*

Originating in Linz (1994), Frenkel's *Body Missing Project* (www.yorku.ca/BodyMissing), an inquiry into the *Kunstraub* (art theft) policies of the Third Reich, has travelled constantly since, most recently to the Freud Museum in London. Her current web-based project, *The Institute*™: *Or, What We Do for Love* (www.the-national-institute.org), has been installed in five Canadian venues, most recently at the National Gallery of Canada in honour of Frenkel's 2006 Governor General's Award for Visual and Media Art.

Frenkel has been artist-in-residence at the School of the Chicago Art Institute, the Slade School of Art, London, the Akademie der Bildende Künste, Vienna, and the Banff School of Fine Arts, among others. Her writings have appeared in numerous art publications, including *artscanada, Art Monthly, Canadian Art, Descant, Fuse, Intermédialités, Public, Vanguard,* and *C Magazine*. Her many honours include the Canada Council Molson Prize, the Bell Canada Award, and the Toronto Arts Award, with honorary degrees from NSCAD (1996) and the Emily Carr Institute of Art and Design (2004). She was elected to the Royal Academy of Arts in 2002, and to the Royal Society in 2006.

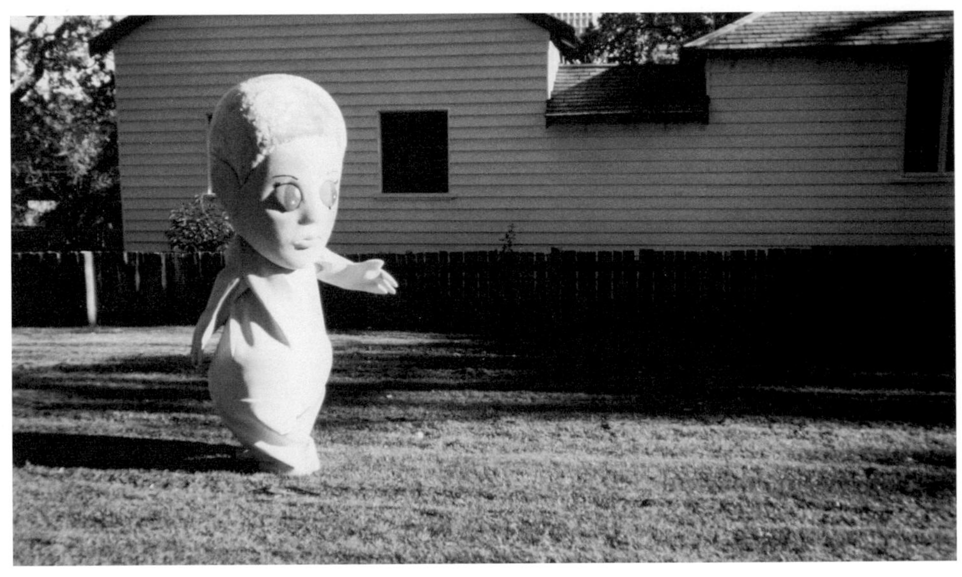

Myfanwy MacLeod (b. 1961, London, Ontario)

The Mascot
1999
Mixed media
Installed: 6 square metres
Collection of Agnes Etherington Art Centre
Purchase, Chancellor Richardson Memorial Fund, 2003
46-046

Untitled (The Mascot)
1999–2001
Framed c print 1/3
78.7 x 106.7 cm
Collection of Agnes Etherington Art Centre
Purchase, Chancellor Richardson Memorial Fund, 2003
46-047

Comics and cartoons have contributed significantly to popular culture(s) around
the world, and it is to this genre of exaggeration, hyperactivity, and fantastic

violence that MacLeod continually turns for inspiration. *The Mascot* relates to her 1997 series *My Idea of Fun* in its humorous but mysterious blend of self-portraiture and cartoon fiction. In this case, MacLeod used animation stills of a naked prepubescent girl (rendered in Japanese anime style) to craft a sculptural cartoon self-portrait, which she then had made into a mascot-like costume.

The costume is "animated" in a photographic print that accompanies it in the gallery space, striding energetically through a suburban backyard. However, in the gallery *The Mascot* is comparatively lifeless: its head detached from a small, deflated body. The oversized head—lying sideways on a sculptural plinth—is open and empty. It is set next to a furry plush club that leans idly in the corner of the gallery space, its function a mystery. Equally ambiguous is the context in which *The Mascot* appears in the photo, where an anonymous inhabitant (perhaps the artist?) acts out a backyard performance that has no other documentation. Amidst the parts, this work is left fragmented both physically and thematically.

The feeling that is left, mixing amusement with unease, is typical of MacLeod's practice. For while much of her work maintains a cartoon's surface exterior and energy, her employment is more deeply layered—disguising dark undertones beneath a comic shell.

Biography

Myfanwy MacLeod was born in London, Ontario, and now lives and works in Vancouver. In 1990 she received an Odette Scholarship from the Toronto Sculpture Garden, which she employed to achieve a BFA at Concordia University in Montreal. In 1994 she moved to Vancouver to complete an MFA at the University of British Columbia, while simultaneously studying at the École Nationale Supérieure des Beaux-Arts in Paris, France. With her studies complete, MacLeod went on to work as both an independent artist and instructor at the Emily Carr Institute of Art and Design in Vancouver. Her recent solo exhibitions include *The Tiny Kingdom*, Or Gallery, Vancouver (2001), *Miss Moonshine*, Catriona Jeffries Gallery, Vancouver (2001), *A Brief Overview of Personology*, Charles H. Scott Gallery, Vancouver (2000), and *How Not to Be Seen*, VTO Gallery, London, UK (2000). Major highlights in group exhibitions include *Relic: New Art from the West Coast*, Fruitmarket Gallery, Edinburgh (2002), *Universal Pictures 3.1*, Blackwood Gallery, Mississauga, and Plug

In ICA, Winnipeg (2001), and *6: New Vancouver Modern*, Morris and Helen Belkin Art Gallery (1998). In 1998 she achieved a VIVA Award from the Doris and Jack Shadbolt Foundation. She is currently represented by the Catriona Jeffries Gallery in Vancouver.

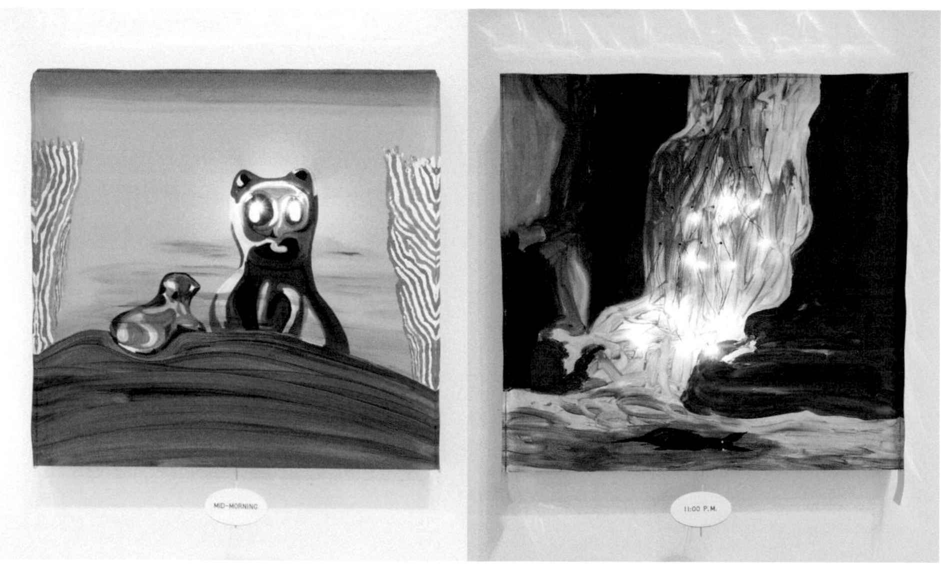

Sandra Meigs (b. 1953, Baltimore, Maryland)
Reckless Days
1997
Oil on masonite with mixed media
8 panels each: 61 x 61 cm
Collection of the Agnes Etherington Art Centre
Purchase, Acquisition Assistance Fund of the Canada Council for the Arts and
Chancellor Richardson Memorial Fund, 2004
47-012

This series of eight paintings was conceived, constructed, and executed within
the frame of an eight-week artist residency in St Jean Port Joli—a small tourist
destination on the St Lawrence River. While staying in this town, living in
the famed Bourgault mansion with its rich interior of baroque woodcarving,
Meigs was drawn to the craft and souvenir shops that line the central roadways.
Within this large collection of cheap knock-offs and kitschy material, she sought
out "meaningful" figurines that would eventually become the central characters of
Reckless Days.

In the translation, eight animal worlds are painted in a folk art style that mixes bright colours, basic composition, and cartoon-like figures. However, despite their dream-like environment and comical feel, each panel communicates anxiety and potential danger.

All eight panels appear under a title banner in the gallery space, and each is labelled with a time of the day (e.g. "3AM," "Dusk," "Midnight"). Despite the labelling, no narrative scheme or chronology governs the order in which they are hung. Adding to this sense of dislocation is the rough surface texture and embedded light bulbs in each panel, which highlight the craft in their construction.

Many of Meigs' painting series are inspired by the real-life travels of the artist, combining her experiences of places like Louisiana, the Florida Everglades, and Boat Basin Farm with compositional structures drawn from film, literature, pop culture, and myth. *Reckless Days* continues this pattern, and the title is drawn largely from a harrowing experience where Meigs almost drowned in a local St Jean Port Joli swimming hole (please see the accompanying artist's statement for more detail). It is with similar ambivalence that the panels of *Reckless Days* work, employing childlike aesthetics to invite the approach of viewers who are subsequently met with complex subject matter.

Artist's Statement

Dear Jan,
Reckless Days came out of an eight-week residency in St Jean Port Joli, *Les Lieux Communs: culture populaire et art contemporain*, curated by Gaston St-Pierre. The time was fast and furious. I had to do research in the area, conceive the idea, construct the panels, and finish the paintings all in that time period.

The strip of highway along St Jean Port Joli was full of small shops selling handmade crafts, a lot of it woodcarving, which had been taught in the area by the Bourgault family, renowned Quebec woodcarvers. The artists all stayed in the Bourgault mansion, which was full of carving: dining room moulding, fireplace moulding, staircase banister; my bed had a carved headboard; there was a statue in the front yard. The rooms were panelled in dark stained wood. Much of the "craft" being sold in these shops had degenerated into a totally kitsch souvenir sentiment.

I spent the first days perusing the shops along the highway. One of the first figurines I saw was a small carved squatting dog. The dog had a small twig (turd) coming out from its bottom. There was one whole glass shelf full of these in replica. The dog with the turd was $5.95. I purchased it. The turd dog appeared in two of the paintings. I continued my quest for meaningful figurines. Most of the *Reckless Days* paintings used the figurines I purchased as inspiration.

One hot, sunny Sunday in July I went with my daughter Ev and Marlene Creates, another resident artist, to what was rumoured to be a nice swimming hole. It was very isolated, down a long trail through the forest. It was a pristine, sublime setting. There was a very high waterfall flowing into a small pond which then cascaded to the valley through another waterfall. It turned out that this pond was a nude pick-up spot for the locals. There were two very gorgeous naked men displaying themselves in serene poses on the top rock of the waterfall overhead. When they saw Ev, who was about four at the time, they modestly retreated. The water was beautiful, and I decided to swim with Ev across the pond to the waterfall so she could get closer to it. It didn't seem that wide a space to traverse. So, with her on my back, I got about halfway across, then realized that I couldn't make it either there or back. I was swimming as well as I could but getting exhausted and could no longer support her. I panicked. I screamed "help, help" as loudly as I could, but the falls muted my voice. I waved one arm frantically, the other holding on to Ev. Marlene finally saw me and swam over to rescue Ev.

With Ev rescued, I sank to the murky bottom. I saw my life flash before my eyes, thinking it was such a stupid way to die, but feeling relieved that Ev was safe. I kind of blanked out. Then I felt this really violent tug on my arm near my shoulder. It was one of the naked men, come to rescue me, after diving down from the top of the waterfall! He dragged me to the shore. I could barely get my breath, having swallowed lots of water. It took me a while to recover enough to walk back to the car. When I got home Marlene had to look after Ev while I cried in my pillow all evening. I was so shaken: I had been so stupid. (My shoulder was sore for months after that.) So my stupidity that day was maybe inspired by those *Reckless Days* paintings which were almost finished by that point. Unfortunately, I never got a chance to thank the naked man for rescuing me.

That painting of the dead deer under the waterfall had been done prior to that experience, and I always think of it as an omen.

So that's the story of the *Reckless Days* paintings! I'm sure there will be more reckless days to come.

Sincerely,
Sandra

Biography

Sandra Meigs was born in Baltimore, Maryland, in 1953, and studied ceramics at the Rhode Island School of Design from 1971–73. Afterward, Meigs moved to Halifax, Nova Scotia, where she achieved a BFA from the Nova Scotia College of Art and Design in 1975, followed by an MA in philosophy from Dalhousie University in 1980. Upon completing her formal education she began to work as a professional artist, as well as instructing at a number of universities and colleges across Canada (including the Banff Centre, the Ontario College of Art and Design, and York University). She currently instructs at the University of Victoria (since 1993), where, in addition to her duties as Professor of Visual Art, she served as Chair of the Visual Arts Department from 1997–2002. Her work has been exhibited across Canada at major institutions, including the Power Plant, the Art Gallery of Ontario, the National Gallery of Canada, and the Ydessa Hendeles Foundation. Internationally, her work has been exhibited at the Freedman Gallery in Reading, Pennsylvania, the Bologna Biennale, the Fifth Biennale of Sydney, and the Fodor Museum, Amsterdam. In addition to her artistic practice, Meigs is a practising filmmaker and published author. She lives and works in Victoria, British Columbia, and is represented by the Susan Hobbs Gallery in Toronto.

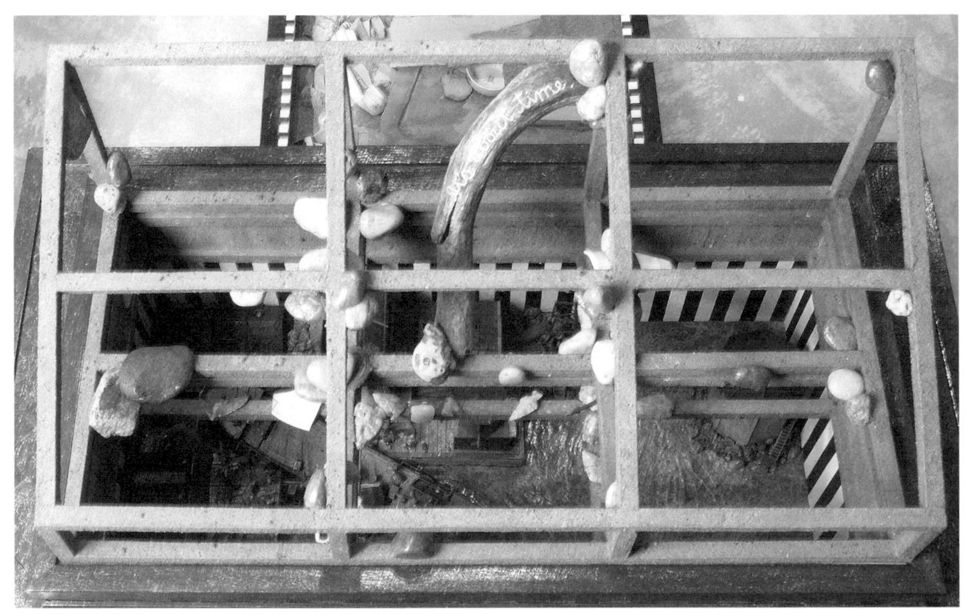

Terry Pfliger (b. 1947, St Joseph, Michigan)
Evolution is but a Long and Complicated Wish … or, it's about Time!
1981
Mixed-media installation
Installed: 160 x 475 x 640 cm
Collection of Agnes Etherington Art Centre
Gift of the Canada Council Art Bank, 2002
45-028

Turning the title into a long, witty pun symptomatic of the humour that flows throughout his practice, Terry Pfliger takes aim at the historical narrative of human evolution in this installation. Composed of nine floor-based boxes laid in a grid before a single, unmanned podium, *Evolution...* quickly assumes the character of a mischievous historian delivering a lecture from on high.

The podium and glass-topped boxes are all filled with dirt, debris, and a selection of domestic objects (i.e. toys, utensils) that Pfliger collects. The vitrine-like boxes mimic the remains of an archaeological dig: the formal presentation and apparent

preservation of a seemingly random collection of junk proposes that each holds valuable traces, evidence supporting an account of our current conditions. Stories begin to unfold within each box. For example, the podium houses a Kingston-inspired scene within an open frame, where a miniature boat attempts to dock at a port city made from clay and train-set props, with disastrous results. In a similar way, each of the nine boxes allows viewers to create their own stories (and histories) from the detritus of civilization.

Pfliger's interest in history (and human construction of it) was first inspired by childhood visits to museums and historic sites in and around Michigan. He takes pleasure in re-creating times and events gone by, stating "I find our whole take on history in this culture a bit humorous and incredibly naïve … so I like playing with it." But rather than using the broad frames of history to explain periods and people in a fixed manner, Pfliger playfully presents his own views of the world to inspire his audience to do the same. He monumentalizes houseflies and hockey players, and plays up the failure of grand aspirations and the prevalence of the accidental. In so doing, he throws open new perspectives on the stories that have shaped our lives, and emphasizes how we continue to shape the world today.

Biography

Terry Lee Pfliger was born in 1947 in St Joseph, Michigan, and earned both his Bachelor of Science and Master of Arts at Western Michigan University between 1965 and 1970. Soon after, he moved to Kingston, Ontario, where he would spend most of the next three decades as both an artist and an instructor. From 1970 to 1973 he taught at Loyalist Collegiate and Vocational College, and from 1973 to 1995 he became a fixture within the art department of St Lawrence College—serving as instructor, program coordinator, and Chair of the Creative Arts Department. During this time Pfliger was also included in numerous solo and group shows across Canada, including *It's About Time*, S.L. Simpson Gallery, Toronto (1982), *Time Bandits*, Artspace Gallery, Peterborough (1986), *Art Bank Works*, National Art Centre, Ottawa, and a 25-year retrospective at the Agnes Etherington Art Centre, *You Can't Get Younger* (1995). His work resides in numerous private collections in Canada and the US, as well as in the public collections of the Agnes Etherington Art Centre and the Canada Council Art Bank. Pfliger has served on the Kingston Artists Association's board of directors, helped found an artists'

co-op in Peterborough (Artspace), and guest-curated *Pfliger's Fancies (Selections from the Permanent Collection)* at the Agnes Etherington Art Centre (1989). In 1995 Pfliger returned to the US where he currently resides as an independent artist in Bridgman, Michigan.

Jill Battson

Jill Battson is an internationally published poet and poetry activist. She has been widely featured in literary journals and anthologies in North America and the UK, and she has performed her work around the globe. Her first book, *Hard Candy*, was nominated for the Gerald Lampert Award. She has written several plays and solo works, including *Ecce Homo*, an enhanced monologue for dance and voice. Battson's most recent book of poems, from Insomniac Press, is *Ashes Are Bone and Dust*.

Steven Heighton

Steven Heighton is the author, most recently, of a novel, *Afterlands,* which recently appeared in Canada and will follow in 2006 in the USA, Britain, Australia, Germany, and the Netherlands. He has also published *The Shadow Boxer,* which was a *Publishers' Weekly* Book of the Year for 2002. His other fiction books are *Flight Paths of the Emperor* and *On earth as it is*, and his poetry collections include *The Ecstasy of Skeptics* and *The Address Book.* His work is translated into nine languages, has been internationally anthologized, and has been nominated for the Governor General's Award, the Trillium Award, a Pushcart Prize, the Journey Prize, and Britain's W.H. Smith Award. He has also won the Lampert Award, the Petra Kenney Prize, the Air Canada Award, and gold medals for fiction and for poetry in the National Magazine Awards. He lives with his family in Kingston, where he is currently working on new poems and translations.

Helen Humphreys

Helen Humphreys is the author of four collections of poetry and four novels. Her most recent book of poetry is *Anthem*, which won the Canadian Authors Association Poetry Award. Her first novel, *Leaving Earth*, won the City of Toronto Book Award and was a *New York Times* Notable Book. Her second novel, *Afterimage*, won the Rogers Writers' Trust Fiction Prize and was also a *New York Times* Notable Book. Her third novel, *The Lost Garden*, was a CBC Canada Reads selection for 2003 and another *New York Times* Notable Book. Her most recent novel is *Wild Dogs*.

Daniel David Moses
Playwright/poet Daniel David Moses hails from the Six Nations Reserve in Ontario. His most recent production was "Songs of Love and Medicine," part of DramFest 2005, produced by the Queen's Drama Department, where he teaches playwriting. His newest publications are *An Anthology of Canadian Native Literature in English* (third edition, Oxford University Press) and *Pursued by a Bear: Talks, Monologues and Tales* (Exile Editions).

Diane Schoemperlen
Born and raised in Thunder Bay, Ontario, Diane Schoemperlen has published several collections of short fiction and two novels, *In the Language of Love* (1994) and *Our Lady of the Lost and Found* (2001). Her collection *Forms of Devotion: Stories and Pictures* won the 1998 Governor General's Award for English Fiction. Her first non-fiction book, *Names of the Dead: An Elegy for the Victims of September 11*, was published in 2004 and was included in *The Globe and Mail*'s 100 Best Books of the Year. Diane Schoemperlen lives in Kingston, Ontario, with her son Alex.

Merilyn Simonds
Merilyn Simonds is the author of twelve books, including *The Convict Lover*, which was a Governor General's Award finalist, and a best-selling collection of linked autobiographical stories, *The Lion in the Room Next Door*. Her most recent work is *The Holding*, a novel published to critical acclaim in 2004 by McClelland & Stewart in Canada and by W.W. Norton in the United States, where it was named a *New York Times* Editor's Choice. She lives near Kingston, Ontario, with writer Wayne Grady.

Carolyn Smart
Carolyn Smart is the author of four volumes of poetry, including *Stoning the Moon* (Oberon Press) and *The Way to Come Home* (Brick Books). In 2001, she published a memoir of her childhood entitled *At the End of the Day* (Penumbra Press). Her forthcoming collection of narrative poems is called *Hooked*. She has lived in the country north of Kingston for more than twenty years and teaches creative writing at Queen's University.

Acknowledgements

This publication is produced in conjunction with the exhibition
Telling Stories, Secret Lives, presented 14 January to 30 April 2006.

Agnes Etherington Art Centre
Queen's University
Kingston, Ontario, Canada K7L 3N6
www.aeac.ca

Curator: Jan Allen
Authors: Jan Allen, Steven Matijcio, with contributing writers Jill Battson,
Steven Heighton, Helen Humphreys, Daniel David Moses, Diane Schoemperlen,
Merilyn Simonds, and Carolyn Smart
Editor: Jan Allen
Copy editor: Steve Anderson
Catalogue design: **WALNUT**
Printing: CJ Graphics Inc., Toronto
Bindery: Anstey Book Binding, Toronto
Distribution: www.ABCartbookscanada.com
Photography: Cheryl O'Brien; p. 3.9 Robin Collyer

© 2006 Agnes Etherington Art Centre, Jan Allen and contributing writers.

This exhibition and publication were made possible by funding from the City of
Kingston's Healthy Community Fund, the Ontario Arts Council, and the Canada
Council for the Arts. The Art Centre acknowledges with gratitude the Chancellor
Richardson Memorial Fund of Queen's University, the Acquisition Assistance
Program of the Canada Council for the Arts, and the donors who support the
continuing development of our contemporary Canadian art collection.

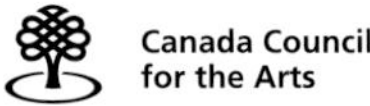

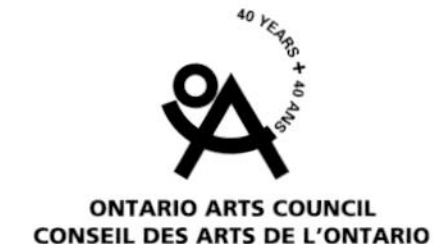

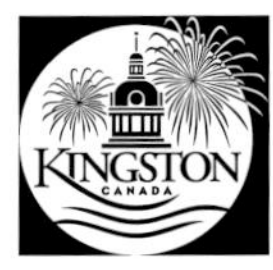

Library and Archives Canada Cataloguing in Publication

Agnes Etherington Art Centre
    Telling stories, secret lives / Jan Allen, Steven Matijcio ; writers: Jill
Battson ... [et al.] ; artists: Dorothy Cameron ... [et al.].

Catalogue to accompany an exhibition held at the Agnes Etherington Art
Centre, Kingston, Ontario, 14 January - 30 April 2006. Installation and
sculptural works from the collection together with responsive stories and poems
written by 7 Kingston writers.

ISBN 1-55339-088-1

    1. Installations (Art)—Canada—Exhibitions. 2. Sculpture, Canadian—
21st century—Exhibitions. I. Allen, Jan, 1952- II. Matijcio, Steven, 1979-
III. Battson, Jill IV. Cameron, Dorothy, 1924-2000. V. Title.

NX430.C32K56 2006   709.71'07471372   C2006-904144-X

Contents

Experiments in Combinatory Aesthetics

Jan Allen

For narrative is not just one form among others. It may be a fundamental structure of thought, like an *a priori* form of sensibility or a category of understanding which allows us to feel and think, and outside of which there is no world, no meaning.

Olivier Asselin[1]

The exhibition *Telling Stories, Secret Lives* was a propositional, thinking-in-public investigation into the meaning and effects of works of art, one that promised to produce interpretive valences squarely outside the restive strictures of contemporary art discourse while respecting in every sense the integrity of the art. Given the show's theme of narrative, and with Olivier Asselin's assertion in mind, it seems most appropriate to offer an account, a story, of the genesis of this exhibition. Also, some observations on its outcome. At first intended to tease forth similarities among works of art that use a similar formal mode—the mode of installational tableaux—a further layer of investigation arose with the invitation of seven writers to contribute responsive texts. This method of establishing connections where they may have been overlooked and, further, fostering the expression of new interpretation concealed a "risk": the possibility of antagonism or displeasure can never be discounted when one goes looking for latent strands of meaning.

When Dorothy Cameron's *The Lost Goddess* was donated to the Art Centre collection, it provoked discussion about how the piece might best be understood within contemporary art practice and within our holdings. A fabulous double self-portrait, the work is an over-the-top illustration of Jungian archetypes rendered in hobbyist materials: self-hardening clay, candles, cardboard, plastic shrimp, and swatches of aquarium foliage. On one level, this intensely private, declamatory tableau is a type of folk shrine or healing fetish. But, even setting aside the body of work of which it is part and the historic contributions of its author, I realized that there are major works in the collection that offer similar tableaux, evoking narrative through the spatial arrangement of allusive components. The delight and shiver of anxiety conjured by Cameron's frank use of symbols and autobiography in *The Lost Goddess* speaks to similar elements in installation art. This resonance of form and content, once observed, raised a question: could an exhibition of these works generate a kind of creative "misreading" and thus prod forward suppressed, yet fundamental, layers of meaning in installation art that has tended to be defined by closed interpretive readings? To what extent can such works be experienced as malleable nodes of cultural expression? The root concept of the show was to position *The Lost Goddess* as precipitant for new meaning in the saturated solution of installation sculpture.

Time has long been understood as a crucial element of installation art insofar as time, and often movement, are required for the viewer to take in the piece; apprehension of the work is thrust into the experiential realm of memory and imagination. Installation art, of course, grew out of Minimalism. Shunning accusations of mere theatricality, installation art staked out other aesthetic claims: its permissible zone of interpretation adhered stubbornly to that regime's twin affirmation of materiality and concept. Fears of facile interpretation led to a reflexive refusal of metaphorical/literary reading, an aversion that seems almost quaint in the light of the frank use of narrative in current art practices. The engine of story—fragmentary in form, recursive, or riven with ambiguity, but nonetheless story—in visual art has seen a renaissance in recent years, a tendency fuelled in part by the inherent temporal motility of proliferating digital media.[2]

While considering this dynamic, I was reminded of the potential of text to invent and expose new facets of visual art by Edward Said's essay "The Art of Displacement: Mona Hatoum's Logic of Irreconcilables." It begins with dreamlike, descriptive passages in which Said ponders the sculptures' literal capacity to function, lending each piece an imagined purpose and agency.[3] He launches his cultural and political reading of the work through a form of sympathetic observation outside art-world interpretive conventions; that is, Said narrativizes the work.

The experiment of the exhibition *Telling Stories, Secret Lives* was thus conceived: we commissioned writers to develop short texts in relation to works of art as a tool to test, and perhaps expand, the interpretive valences of seven mixed-media installations from our contemporary art collection. The first question or hypothesis was: in the modular art work in which, to a greater or lesser degree, space becomes time, to what extent is narrative invoked? Seven writers were each given an open-ended invitation to view a specific work and submit a short responsive text: the expectation was not that they write about the work of art, nor articulate its content, but rather engage with the artwork as prompt for a parallel production. A secondary hypothesis comes into play: how do two well-developed creators working in different disciplines encounter one another through their respective productions? Of course, in this case, there was a vector: the artists were not afforded a riposte. The outcome was an exhibitionary twinning of major art and writing, so a third layer of experimentation resulted at the level of the audience: would the presence of texts clearly outside curatorial authority produce a different type of social situation in the gallery?

The invited writers, all very accomplished, were poets, novelists, and playwrights, but the form of written expression was left open to them. While several of the writers had previously written in response to art, for most such a directed request was alien to their normal writing process. Nonetheless, they all gamely took up the task.

The "secret lives" portion of the exhibition title suggests the way we hide from one another, and that the sheer richness of individual consciousness is unimaginably more specific and complex than can ever be fully expressed. So much remains submerged—invisible, inaccessible even to ourselves—about the impulses, feelings, and realities of our lives. The exhibition proposed that works of art, too, have a secret life, a reservoir of untapped meaning.

This territory of the hidden, elusive aspects of character, both private and public, underpins Vera Frenkel's *Her Room in Paris (The Secret Life of Cornelia Lumsden: A Remarkable Story, Part 1)*. The work is an elaborate machine of staged suggestion, splintering arguments, contradictions, anachronisms, and playfully constructed coincidence, presented in the purported famous author's hastily abandoned "Room in Paris." Helen Humphreys' brief, eloquent poem in response to Frenkel's piece is an affecting counterpoint. The restraint and lucid tenor of Humphreys' poem conjure a still point of reflection that stands apart from the teasing social dimension of Frenkel's fictive character, the calculatedly haphazard reconstruction of her last known whereabouts, and the videotaped record of dubious testimonials. While expanding upon a core theme of *The Secret Life of Cornelia Lumsden*, Humphreys' piece exposes its method of accrued incident and evasion, while pointing to the universally corrosive disregard of time for vanity.

A similar contrast of voice, to very different effect, develops in Steven Heighton's poem responding to Myfanwy MacLeod's *The Mascot*. Naked but armed, isolated and swollen-headed, *The Mascot* is an anime-eyed cartoon mascot of the human condition, redolent with the charms of pop culture and the endless appetites of consumerism. Heighton crafted an interior monologue for the character, filling that empty head with nothing less than an elegy for the body, recounting an anguished history of civilization, of humanity's love affair with information and attendant abandonment of the physical body in favour of the ballooning info corpus. The lavish language and incantation of historical and literary allusion in Heighton's poem are hilariously at odds with the serene vacuity of *The Mascot*'s form.

Ian Carr-Harris' *The Anchor Bible, "Judith"; A New Translation with Introduction and Commentary by Carey A. Moore (Garden City, N.Y., 1985), 23* offers a doubling, presenting two tables, each bearing a representation of the apocryphal story of Judith and Holofernes, a tale vividly entrenched in the Western cultural imagination. Inspired by scientific evidence of seconds of awareness experienced by the beheaded, Merilyn Simonds elegantly layers description of these moments with an imagined dialogue between the euphoric Judith and the dying Holofernes. Like Steve Heighton, Simonds chose to render the thoughts of the subject. Holofernes, in his last, flickering shreds of consciousness, predicts the inevitable unity of heroine and victim: with the success of Judith's courage and duplicity, Holofernes' death binds them for all time. Simonds thus invents the first telling—an eyewitness account—of this tale, extending the logic of Carr-Harris' intentions, while observing that history simultaneously fulfils and defeats intention.

The theme of history and its apprehension likewise suffuses Terry Pfliger's *Evolution is but a Long and Complicated Wish ... or, It's about Time!* in which nine low boxes of detritus are arranged in a grid, reminiscent of an archeologist's dig, before an altar-like podium containing ceramic tableaux. Mating her own favoured stylistic device with the modular form of Pfliger's installation, the core of Diane Schoemperlen's text is a ten-part list of clustered sentences in which the elements in each sculptural segment are animated. Schoemperlen imagines the domestic objects in use, describing the minor accidents—not cataclysms—that damaged them, while conjuring up the North American middle class of the 1950s in her poignant rendering of the small disasters of daily life and, especially, its endearing persistence. Aligning herself with the giddy but dark humour of Pfliger's work, Schoemperlen posits evolution not as progress but rather as resilience sustained by fleeting scenarios of observed beauty in the face of sequential loss. If Pfliger is staging entropy, Schoemperlen's counter gesture is to breathe life into the elements, artist and writer each counting, in their own sweet way, on the redemptive yearning of the "complicated wish."

Robin Collyer's *Megaphone* is the least modular work in *Telling Stories, Secret Lives*: its elements are abutted such that the piece may be read as a unitary sculpture of interpenetrating parts. It is distinct in its degree of abstraction: the suppression of detail and re-orientation of the forms' architectural referents offered wide interpretive scope for writer Daniel David Moses. The resulting "BIG NOISE" reads *Megaphone* as the altar for a religion of abstract beliefs, a religion bereft of the messy world—with its textures and ambiguities—eschewing even the particularities of dogma. Here monochrome abstract form stands for the values of rationalist thought, sufficient to itself and ultimately life-depleting, however comforting its suppressions might be. The charming sense of movement and warm precision of language in Moses' poem do little to disguise his unease with the authoritarian serenity of Collyer's *Megaphone*.

Carolyn Smart's text is a short piece of prose that takes as its jumping off point the artist's account of a dramatic incident associated with the making of the eight-part painting *Reckless Days*: a near drowning. Meigs' work and the aesthetic sensibility embedded in it functioned as prompts for Smart's own memories. In "When I was young," she lays out a cluster of characters, anxieties, and events that wonderfully capture the complex distortions and vulnerabilities of childhood perception. Truly a parallel production to *Reckless Days*, Smart's story does not attempt to track the events depicted in Meigs' piece; but the pitch of faux naïve voice is a perfect literary equivalent of the work's acrid chroma, broad facture, scatological protrusions, twinkly lights, and trailing mylar flanges. Smart's story also echoes the fragmented temporality of Meigs' piece; events are not harnessed in causal relationships; they read outside linear chronology as a series of illuminated tableaux.

Jill Battson's approach to Dorothy Cameron's *The Lost Goddess* was to take the self portrait as an invitation to research the woman behind the work, a flamboyant gallerist and mainstay of the 1960s Toronto art scene, who began making art late in life. Battson interviewed the late artist's husband, painter Ronald Bloore, and pored through snapshots of their life together. This intensive process generated a cycle of seven poems out of which "Fishy Business" emerged as the piece of choice for *Telling Stories, Secret Lives*. The poem is a declaration of purpose from the point of view of the subject. Yet another history unfurls: in Battson's account, a traumatic lineage of giving birth to the divine culminates with the bizarre delivery of a beady-eyed shrimp as armoured emblem of feminine power. A stately kind of tenderness seeps through the text as Battson conjures the raucous, exasperated vulnerability of *The Lost Goddess*.

Can one hope to draw conclusions from such an experiment in combinatory aesthetics? Observations, to be sure. It can be said that the capacity of these particular works of art to engage in current and evolving conditions, in which their meanings will surely be renegotiated by successive publics, was exercised. What is more, *Telling Stories, Secret Lives* went some way toward animating the public art gallery as a social space. The project's inference of the collective formation of meaning of the work of art was not lost on our audiences. A community of viewer/readers was generated in the gallery by the presence of these compelling and (for the exhibition space) idiosyncratic texts: they set up a zone of conviviality, encouraging conversation, return visits, and the bringing of guests. In attempting to understand installation art as scenario, and by bringing in the outsider/literary voice, the show placed value on inter-subjectivity over sheer opticality, or—perhaps better—made explicit their tethering. In the combination of productions from different creative disciplines, the relationship within each participant/object dyad may be alliance or sympathy, but, as we saw above, may well be antagonistic. As theorist of installation art Claire Bishop argues, the oppositional dynamic may be most revealing, most valuable, for its ability to demarcate and vigorously expand the psychological space surrounding the work of art.[4]

Notes

1 Olivier Asselin, "Narrative and Navigable Space and Databases: A Few Remarks on Digital Cinema," *raconte moi/tell me* (Québec: Musée national des beaux-arts du Québec, 2005), p. 117.

2 For example, see Marie Fraser, "Tell Me, or The Narrative and Its Paradoxes," *raconte moi/tell me.*

3 Edward Said, "The Art of Displacement: Mona Hatoum's Logic of Irreconcilables," in *Mona Hatoum: The Entire World as a Foreign Land* (London: Tate Gallery, 2000), pp. 7–17.

4 Claire Bishop, "Antagonism and Relational Aesthetics," *October*, vol. 110 (Fall 2004), pp. 51–79.